Successful Parties

and

How To Give Them

D1553426

By MARJORIE WACKERBARTH
and
LILLIAN S. GRAHAM

BAKER BOOK HOUSE
Grand Rapids, Michigan

ISBN: 0-8010-9550-6

Library of Congress Catalog Card Number: 61-9689

TO

James II, Bob, Graham,
Frank, Carl, and James I

Foreword

Parties are an important part of every youngster's growth and development. They are not only good fun but they teach youngsters the joy of entertaining, and how to be good hosts and hostesses.

Unfortunately few people are born with the knack of giving a good party. And many parents sorely feel their lack when it is time for their first born to celebrate his birthday.

This book is planned to help those who want their children to learn the art of social entertainment. Good parties don't just happen. They are planned so that there will be no wallflowers and no dull moments.

The seventy-one parties in this book are complete from invitations to goodbyes for lads and lassies from tiny tots through adolescence. Each party is planned around a central theme, and this theme is carried throughout the evening. The games show how familiar games often can be tailored to fit a special theme.

The four hundred games used in these parties are completely indexed in the back of the book so that the book can be used as a game book as well as a party book.

A group of parties is offered for the lassies who want strictly "girl-parties." A large group of practical parties that have proved themselves successful is offered for the in-between-age boy, the lad often socially neglected because his parties seem to be hard to plan.

None of these parties calls for expensive or elaborate equipment and all of them have been tried out. So give a party and have fun.

Acknowledgments

We gratefully acknowledge permission from the following magazines to reprint these stories which we have written for them.

American Home
>Birthdays Must Be Celebrated
>A Party for Boisterous Boys
>A Stag for Thirteeners
>A Teen-Age Party
>The Goblins Will Get You

Calling All Girls
>Flowers in February
>Twelfth-Night Party

Christian Mother
>Start with Starch
>Party for Tricycle Set

Christian Science Monitor
>Add Some Spice

Country Gentleman
>Make It a Family Affair

>>Reprinted by special permission from Country Gentleman magazine, copyright, 1949, by The Curtis Publishing Company.

Farm Journal
>The First Boy-Girl Party
>Kiddie Cat Prowl
>Rainbow's Pot of Gold

Contents

Fun for the Very Young

FUN FOR THE SMALL FRY

If your tiny-tot has a birthday soon, celebrate the event with a party. The little people at this starry-eyed age are easy to please with a variety of activities.

One of the most attractive birthday parties our small one ever attended was held from three to five P.M. This gave Tad plenty of time to have his nap so he went to the party well refreshed. Because of the youth of the guests we mothers were invited too. However, when we arrived our individual responsibility ceased for the afternoon.

The dining room which joined the living room had been cleared of as much furniture as possible. Small tables and chairs borrowed from a nearby church nursery were scattered about. Large sheets of brown wrapping paper for would-be artists were piled on the end of one table. Nearby were plenty of crayons. Bright-colored magazines (old ones) and plenty of round-pointed shears —also borrowed from nursery school—were handy.

A big box of nursery blocks and all available toys owned by the small host were in this same room. Everything was ready when the small guests arrived. This was the children's room—the mothers stayed in the adjoining living room, close enough to oversee the youngsters yet far enough away so the youngsters felt free.

It was fun to watch the small fry. The little chairs were

inspected first. One or two such chairs at home were no novelty but here was a whole roomful. They needed to be looked over, sat in and moved about. Soon even the shyest child was busy playing. The older tykes began drawing or cutting and soon the younger ones were following suit.

After a period of free play the young host's mother produced a tiny bell and asked the children if they wouldn't like to play "Ring Bell Ring." All the children bowed their heads in their laps while Johnny, holding on to the bell clapper, ran and hid in the next room. When he was safely hidden the hostess called out, "Ring Bell Ring." The children then pointed in the direction of the bell ringer. This simple game delighted the children and had to be repeated again and again with a different bell ringer each time.

Then the hostess told a story about Mother Kitty and Baby Kitty. She chose a little lass to be Mother Kitty. Then Mother Kitty and all the baby kitties went fast asleep. While Mother Kitty slept four of the babies awakened and tiptoed away to hide. When Mother Kitty awakened and found her babies gone she cried, "Meow." The little lost kittens cried, "Mew." Mother Kitty had to locate her babies by sound. After her every "Meow," the babies answered, "Mew."

"Policeman and Lost Child" next delighted the youngsters. One child was Policeman, and Mother worriedly asked his help in searching for her lost child. The Policeman asked Mother to tell him what her lost child was wearing. Mother then described in detail the clothes of her lost child. The Policeman looked about at the children and brought to Mother the child answering the description.

A "Game of Touch" was next on the program. The hostess put three familiar objects in a cloth bag—a ball, a toy automobile and a pencil. Each youngster took his turn at identifying the objects by feeling them through the bag. For "Bucket Ball" the children formed a circle with a wastebasket in the center. Then each child was given a chance to throw a large rubber ball into the wastebasket. Young children are not very adept at aiming a ball, but they thoroughly enjoy ball games. In this game, if a youngster did get the ball in the basket he was given another throw.

Blowing bubbles is always tops in fun. This wise hostess placed a low flat pan in the center of one of the low tables. In it she had put a mixture of soapy water and a few drops of glycerin. She gave each child a straw. Soon the air was filled with squeals of delight from the youngsters as the bubbles floated upward. The straws were excellent blowers, made no mess, and were easily replaced when broken by chubby fingers.

After the activity of these games the youngsters were ready to settle down at the tables to try finger painting. Each child was fitted with a large paper apron to protect his party clothes. The bib-style aprons were made of heavy butcher's paper on which ties and halters of tape had been stitched. Finger painting of course is that familiar childhood art of smearing finger paint onto large sheets of paper with the fingers. Our hostess made a generous supply of three colors of finger paint. Here is her recipe.

Dissolve one-eighth cup of laundry starch in a half cup of cold water. Slowly add to a pint of boiling water and cook about five minutes stirring constantly to keep the mixture smooth. Add vegetable coloring and let cool. For this party the hostess had divided the mixture into three parts—coloring one red, the second green, and the third blue. These were then put into little cold-cream jars so that each child could choose a color and work individually. It saved much scrapping over jars.

Our hostess, knowing that nothing upsets young children's schedules more than party refreshments in late afternoon, solved the difficulty by serving a simple supper shortly before five o'clock. A gaily decorated paper tablecloth transformed the play-table into a festive board.

A big bunch of brightly colored balloons was fastened to the chandelier which hung directly over the center of the table, just out of reach of small groping hands. Each child was given a crown of stiff paper to wear. The crowns were all alike except the birthday child's which was decorated with three paper candles.

The menu was simple and in keeping with tiny-tot diets. Each plate held baked potato in half shell, a helping of buttered peas and a mold of fruit Jello. The dessert consisted of ice cream and the birthday cake. The cake held three candles. When the young host tried to blow them out he received a great deal of help from his guests.

To the youngsters, many of whom at home were in the habit of eating in a high chair and wearing a bib, it was a delight to be sitting at a table with a group of their own age. Plates were cleaned in surprisingly short order.

At Good-bye time the balloons were untied from the chandelier and given one to each child. This was one Tiny-tot party that was enjoyed not only by the wee ones but the mothers as well. We blessed our thoughtful hostess when we tumbled our tired, happy, well-fed youngsters into bed and served the family dinner without interruption.

THE FIRST PARTY!

Will your "So-Big" be three years old his next birthday? What fun to give him his first birthday party! He'll talk about it days beforehand and play party for many days after. That is, if he has enjoyed his first party. And he is sure to if you plan it properly.

Parties for these small fry need not, and should not be elaborate affairs that cost a lot of money. His guests should be a small group of his own friends—not limited to the children of your friends. And it should be carefully planned to avoid any youngster upsets the following day.

In the first place, nothing upsets the schedules of small children more than party refreshments in the late afternoon. An early supper solves the refreshment problem. And their mothers will be grateful indeed because on arriving home the tired children can all be popped into bed immediately and the family dine undisturbed.

From three to five o'clock are the best party hours for small children. Three o'clock doesn't interfere with nap time, thus allowing each child his undisturbed rest and putting him in good spirits for the party. Since parties for children under six years of age should never last more than two hours each, small guests will have abundant time for play and will be ready for home by five o'clock.

If because of transportation difficulties mothers must

be included, ask them to bring their darning. They should
have a separate place in which to visit so they may not be
annoyed by the youngsters' activities nor be tempted to
interrupt the children's play.

Party entertainment for these little kiddies must be
quite different from that of older children. These small
fry do not visit like adults, therefore something must be
prepared ahead of time to occupy each guest as soon as he
arrives.

For this very special party, whenever it is possible, clear
a room of big pieces of furniture. In place of the grown-
ups' dining table substitute a long, low children's table.
Such a table and accompanying chairs can be borrowed
from a nearby Sunday school or library room. This im-
provised playroom will delight even the shyest child. If a
few small cars or a doll or two are out on the table to
interest the early arrivals, a trying moment of the first
party will be bridged.

As soon as all the little tousle-heads have arrived, be
ready to start the program of games. By all means, and
this is so important, have all activities for the afternoon
planned with not the slightest detail left to chance.

Seat the guests around the table and give each one a
sheet of white construction paper upon which you have
previously drawn or traced the outline of some animal—
an elephant, a cat, or a dog. Pass a box of colored crayons,
one for each child, to be used to color his animal. If the
child can't keep his coloring inside the lines, ignore it—
he'll enjoy the coloring just as much as if he did.

When the children have finished the coloring to their
satisfaction, give them round-tipped scissors with which
to cut out the pictures they have colored. The youngsters
will be very proud of their animals and will love lining
them up on the mantel for exhibition. You'll find the
children returning again and again to the mantel to ad-

mire their handiwork. Of course, each child will take home his own colored animal.

After this concentrated effort the youngsters will enjoy a story. Pick a simple story like *William and His Kitten,* by Marjorie Flack (Houghton). Assign to each child one of the characters of the story. For instance, let Tommy be the kitten, and every time the kitten is mentioned in the story, Tommy mews. One child may be the postman, another the grocer, etc. When the postman is mentioned, the boy having that part whistles, the grocer says, "humph." With a bit of ingenuity you can find something for each child to do. When you read the story slow up a bit as you come to the characters, thus giving each child time to realize his turn has come. This makes the story much more exciting to the young participants and holds the attention of even the most active.

After the story these little ones will want to move about a bit. "Drop the Handkerchief" is a good game, and the children will especially enjoy it if accompanied by a song. All the players except the one who is "IT" stand in a circle. Encourage the children to sing the old favorite "A Tisket, A Tasket" with you, as "IT" runs around the outside of the circle carrying a hanky. At the words "I dropped it," "IT" drops the hanky behind a player. As soon as this player discovers the hanky behind him he

A Tisket, A Tasket

A   tis-ket, a tas-ket, a green and yel-low bas-ket, I

sent a let-ter to my love, and on the way I dropped it.

quickly picks it up and runs around the circle trying to catch "IT" before he reaches the vacant place in the circle. For small children it is better to let each one take a turn at being "IT" rather than insisting that "IT" be caught each time.

After this active game the children will enjoy a finger play. "Five Little Squirrels" was always a favorite with our small lads.

> Five little squirrels lived up in a tree.
> Said the first little squirrel, "What do I see?"
> Said the second little squirrel, "Let's have some fun."
> Said the third little squirrel, "I smell a gun."
> Said the fourth little squirrel, "Let's hide in the shade."
> Said the fifth little squirrel, "I'm not afraid."
> When "Bang" went the gun
> And away they did run.

It is well first to show the children the game. Then repeat it and let them do it with you. It is played this way. Start with each hand doubled into a fist. When the first squirrel speaks, the little fingers rise; when the second squirrel speaks, the fourth fingers rise; the third squirrel, the third fingers and so on until the thumbs rise when the fifth squirrel speaks. At the word "Bang" clap your hands and on the last line quickly put them behind your back. If you're not already familiar with the words, memorize the verse and actions so that the children can follow you without hesitation. The youngsters will love this game and want to repeat it again and again.

Just before time to eat bring on paper crowns made of gay-colored construction paper, one for each child. The birthday child's can differ from the others in that it can be cut across the front to represent three candles. While the children are trying on and admiring their crowns, cover the low table with a paper tablecloth and matching napkins. For the table centerpiece use gay balloons on sticks thrust in a vase.

The youngsters will adore the bright table with only their own friends eating with them. Children greatly prefer foods that are familiar to them so it is foolish to spend hours preparing an elaborate meal. Meat loaf, baked potato and creamed carrots or peas are foods that will satisfy most children. And, of course, the inevitable ice cream and cake will finish the meal.

After supper each guest is given one of the balloons to take home with him along with his crown and his colored animal. When you see all the happy little guests so proud of their possessions and hear your own child prattle about his party, you'll know that the party has been a success and well worth every bit of effort you have put into it.

PARTY FOR
THE TRICYCLE SET

When your youngster stands "knee-high to a grasshopper," and is looking forward to this third or fourth birthday, nothing is so much fun for both mother and child as planning and giving a party. For at this wide-eyed age birthdays must be celebrated.

Important in making a joyful occasion is the planning. The games, the food, the hours, and the tempo of the party must be tailored-made for the young host and guests.

When our lads were small we discovered that two hours was the ideal length of time for a party. In this length of time the young host and his guests had ample time to play the games, eat a hearty lunch, and leave for home before anyone was exhausted enough to have reached the "squally stage." From three o'clock to five o'clock are the ideal hours. At this time the party won't interfere with nap time nor run into the dinner hour.

If you have an amusement room, that's ideal, but if not choose one room and confine your "party" to that room. Everyone will be happier than if the youngsters chase all over the house. Remove precious bric-a-brac, and move in as much small furniture as possible. Sometimes it's wise to borrow small chairs and tables from a neighborhood nursery or church Sunday School. Little folks adore furniture their own size. But if you can't get small furniture, let the youngsters sit on the floor. They do it in nursery schools and kindergartens so why not at a party?

As to entertainment take a tip from nursery schools and plan simple games that will include the entire group.

A good starter is called Roll the Ball. The children sit in a circle with feet spread apart so that each child touches the foot of the child next to him on either side. If the ball rolls into his garage — made by his feet — he must roll the ball to another garage. The youngsters think this is a lot of fun. After they have become used to the idea of the game, then it can change to Hot Ball. Pretend that the ball is hot and it must be moved as quickly as possible.

It is wise to watch your players and see that they are not tiring. Their span of interest at this age is short.

For a change of pace try Skip Tag. The children stand in a circle, each child holding his hands behind him. Choose one child to skip around the circle and touch some child's hand. The child touched then skips around the circle in opposite direction until he meets the first child. The children then make a turn-about — the first child then returning to the empty space in the circle. The second child then skips on around the circle and touches a third child, etc. Occasionally a little child has not learned to skip. If not, let that youngster trot around the circle.

Skip Tag is more fun with music. Humming a simple march is suitable, or a phonograph record can be used. Of course, if some one can play a piano so much the better.

If in the course of play a youngster should take a tumble, tears are quickly forgotten, if Mother starts the rhyme:

> Hurrah for Bobby Bumble!
> He never minds a tumble,
> But up he jumps and rubs his bumps,
> And doesn't even grumble!

The youngsters almost immediately catch on and will repeat the verse with Mother, much to the enjoyment of all, even the fallen one.

"Little Tommy Tittlemouse" is tops with most children. One child hides behind a big chair where he can't be seen. A second child stands in front of the chair while the group sings:

Little Tommy Tittlemouse sat in a little house,
Someone's knocking, Oh me, Oh my,
  (The child in front knocks on the chair)
Someone's calling —
  (The child knocking says, "It is I.")

The youngster in hiding must recognize the caller by his voice. It is amazing how quickly little children can do this.

Another standard nursery school game that fits well into a home party is Bouncing Ball. The children stand in a circle and try to bounce the ball into a popcorn can 'or wastebasket. If the ball goes in, the group all clap in approval. This simple game is greeted with enthusiasm.

For a quiet time before eating, the children love to say together little kindergarten verses. If your party is in the winter these are appropriate.

JACK FROST

B-r-r-r! It's very cold today
B-r-r-r! Jack Frost is out at play
He pinches through my heavy clothes;
He bites my cheeks and nips my nose.
B-r-r-r! It's very cold today.
Jack Frost is out at play.

A child thinks it fun to nip his own nose with his fingers when he repeats the appropriate line.

SNOW FLAKES

The snow flakes are falling by one's and by two's
There's snow on my jacket, there's snow on my shoes.
There's snow on the bushes, there's snow on the trees.
There's snow on everything now, if you please!

Everyone who has ever had children knows how hard it is to feed a tired child whose appetite was spoiled by late refreshments. Instead of refreshments it is much wiser to give an early simple supper to the little guests and let them be ready for bed when they get home. Their mothers will bless you.

Children prefer simple foods they are familiar with, so serve a small helping of mashed potatoes, a vegetable, and a fruit jello, topped off with the traditional birthday cake and ice cream.

Just before going home is the time to give favors — a balloon, a whistle (big enough not to swallow) or a sucker.

Your youngster will play party for days, we promise. And this will be your thanks and proof that he has enjoyed his very own home party.

BIRTHDAYS MUST BE CELEBRATED

The secret of entertaining small children successfully is to have a variety of activities, none of which lasts too long. Children adore making things; kindergartners as well as older children. At a recent five-year-old's birthday party the children made small paper baskets, which pleased them much more than any ready-made baskets. Here is how they are made.

Bright-colored construction paper is the most attractive to use. For the basket proper the paper is cut in squares six by six inches. Then crease the paper into sixteen small squares by folding it in half four times. On two opposite sides slit the corner squares to the first crease. These corner squares are folded over and pasted on to the two end center squares, forming the ends of the basket. The handles are also cut out of the same colored paper. They can be five or six inches long and about one-half inch in width. A cut-out paper animal or fowl can be used for decoration.

The baskets are pasted first, then the handles pasted on and the little decorations pasted on last. Little scissors are provided and the guests fringe the edges of the baskets.

Spread out upon a table the cut and folded paper for the baskets, handles, and decorations. Let each child make his own choice of color for his basket, handle, and ornament, and then paste them together. This may sound difficult but it is not. The children love to make the baskets and you'll have a big surprise at the good-looking baskets. When the baskets are finished place them on the mantel where they can be admired and later filled with candy to be taken home. Older children may be permitted to make the initial cuts and folds for the baskets.

Little children like to play familiar games. "Going to Jerusalem" is an old standby. For this game line up a row of small chairs or stools, backs together—one for each guest. The children march around the chairs to the music. While they are marching remove one chair. The instant the music stops everyone scrambles for a seat. The child left without a chair then sits on the side lines while the same procedure is repeated. The one holding the last chair is declared the winner. We find that if the group all clap for the winner it leaves a better feeling than if prizes are awarded.

"Dropping Clothespins into a Bottle" is another delightful game for small youngsters. Remember it? Place a milk bottle on the floor back of a straight chair. The youngster kneels on the chair facing the back. Then he is given five or six clothespins to drop into the bottle, one at a time. Each child keeps track of the number he can get into the bottle. The winner is cheered.

Every child loves a motion song. One that our older boys learned at camp delighted our group. The words are rather silly and the motions sillier but that's part of the fun. Each child puts his thumbs to his ears with the fingers free—donkey fashion. Then all sing to the tune of "Turkey in the Straw."

Do your ears hang low?   *With thumbs to ear, wave fingers.*

Do they wobble to and fro?	*Hands together in front, waving back and forth.*
Can you tie them in a knot?	*Go through motions of tying a knot.*
Can you tie them in a bow?	*More motions of tying.*
Can you sling them over your shoulder?	*Sling folded hands over shoulder.*
Like a continental soldier?	*Salute.*
Do your ears hang low?	*Hands wobbling at ears.*

The song starts slowly and with each repetition gets faster, finally ending in a burst of hilarity.

Other games accompanied by songs such as "London Bridge" (London Bridge is falling down) and "Drop the Handkerchief" (A tisket, a tasket, a green and yellow basket. I sent a letter to my love and on my way I dropped it) are very popular.

"Button, button, who has the button?" and "I Spy" also are fun. All of these games require no expensive equipment and keep the youngsters happy.

A birthday cake and ice cream or sherbet complete the birthday party. At this time bring the baskets to the table and fill them with small candies. The children are proud to take home baskets they have made themselves.

Suckers, tied with gay streamers of crepe paper to the dining-room chandelier, give the room a festive air, and also can be given the youngsters to take home.

Take a bit of your busy time in these hurried days and help the little people celebrate the important days. It pays big dividends.

For Lassies

GRANDMOTHER FOR A DAY

"I'm tired of always being the youngest in the family," sputtered the rebellious Linda one day.

Her mother laughed at her crossness and then had an idea.

"How would you like to be a grandmother for a day?" she asked.

Linda forgot her crossness and brightened up, "How?" "How could I?"

"We could plan a Grandmother's party and invite your friends in for an afternoon tea like Grandmother used to enjoy when she was young."

And this was the start of Linda's "Grandmother's" party. To give her invitations an old-fashioned touch Linda pasted colored rickrack braid around the edges of small white cards. On the cards she printed "Come to Linda's for Grandmother's Day."

When her excited guests arrived they were directed to the back bedroom where they found two large boxes—one filled with old long dresses, one for each little guest—the other filled with hats, gloves, beads, and other fancies.

Around the room Linda had pinned a few old-fashioned pictures which the girls studied to get ideas about hair styles. Also they were not familiar with the black court-plaster beauty spots until they saw an old photograph.

After considerable hilarity over "dressing-up" and a proper time devoted to primping, Linda announced a style show to discover the prettiest costume, the funniest, and the cleverest. Winners would be judged by the applause of the guests and awarded prizes.

After all this excitement the girls went to the living room for a "Quilting Bee," so popular when Grandmother was a girl. Each girl was given a small square of tarlatan and enough tiny squares of gay cotton material to cover it—also a tube of glue. Each girl then glued her cotton squares to the tarlatan back to make a doll-sized quilt. The girl with the nicest looking quilt was awarded a prize.

Because even interested girls do not like to sit still too long, the next game was an active one. Linda put a work basket in the center of the floor and around it circles of various colored tissue paper which represented balls of Grandmother's yarn. Each girl was then given a cardboard fan (Manila folders make good fans). Then each girl tried for one minute to fan as many balls of yarn as possible into the work basket. Linda's mother timed each contestant and awarded a small prize to the most successful. This game is very tricky because the thin paper blows out of the basket as easily as it blows in.

In Grandmother's childhood homemade feather beds and pillows were common in every home, so Linda planned a feather relay. Her guests were divided into two groups. The first player of each group was given a feather. Each girl keeps her feather in the air by blowing on it while she crosses the room and returns. She then hands her feather to the next in line. The side finishing first wins the relay.

The next game was "Grandma." Linda was the first Grandma and stood with her face to the wall. The other players stood in a line across the room. The idea of the game is for the players to creep up on Grandma without being seen. Grandma could turn at any time to look over her left shoulder or her right shoulder, but she could not at any time turn all the way around. If Grandma caught sight of a player moving she sent her back to the starting point. The player who first was able to creep up on Grandma and touch her took Linda's place and became the next Grandma.

Teatime came all too quickly. It consisted of thin nut-bread sandwiches cut with fancy cookie cutters, and cocoa. Old-fashioned snowballs and plenty of ice cream satisfied the sweet tooth. Snowballs, so popular in Grandmother's day, are squares of white cake frosted on all sides with white cocoanut frosting.

Linda and her guests all decided that having a "Grandmother's" party was lots of fun.

FLOWERS IN FEBRUARY

Nancy pressed her nose against the windowpane, as she watched the swirling snow outside. "I'll bet it blizzards on my birthday again this year. Almost every February is the same. Just once I'd like to have a birthday party in the summer time."

Nancy's mother looked up from her sewing with a smile. "Why not pretend it's summer and invite your friends over on your birthday for a summertime party?"

"Oh — what fun!" Nancy's eyes danced with delight, then she grew sober. "We couldn't play outdoors."

"No, but I think we could plan an indoor summer party that would be fun on a cold February day. Let's put on our thinking caps."

That was the beginning of Nancy's summer party. She decided to make it a flower party and to use Brown-eyed Susans for the invitations. These she cut from yellow construction paper. A little brown center completed the flower. Across the petals she wrote:

> Come to a flower party
> Friday at three P. M.
> At Nancy's house,
> 805 Blunt Street

Naturally Nancy's friends were curious about a flower party in February. Garden parties in summer, of course, but this was different. It sounded like fun.

As the guests arrived Nancy gave each one a card on which the guest wrote her initials, such as B.F.V., or

S.B.N. After everyone had arrived Nancy asked the girls to trade cards with each other. Then she directed that they write the name of a flower beginning with the last initial, and two descriptive words beginning with the first two initials, such as B.F.V. Big Fat Violet — S.B.N. Sun-Burned Nasturium.

When this was finished the cards were returned to the original holder. Each girl then read the flowery interpretation of her own initials.

For the next game called "Flowers" the girls sat in a circle. Nancy explained that the first girl should name a flower beginning with the letter "A" such as "Aster." The second should repeat the first flower named and add one beginning with "B" such as "Aster, Bluebell." The third one should repeat the first two flowers named and add one beginning with "C," so on around the circle and through the alphabet.

If a player could not think of a flower beginning with the correct letter, or slipped up on correctly repeating the list given she withdrew and sat outside the circle. The game continued until only two players were left. These were captains for the next game.

To tie in with the flower theme Nancy called the next relay "Seeds." The group divided into two lines headed by the two captains. A small pile of navy beans (seeds) was placed on a table in front of each line. Each player was given a straw. At the word "go" the two captains ran forward, sucked a bean firmly onto the *end* of their straw and ran across the room depositing the bean in a glass. The line that got the most beans transferred from the pile to the glass won. If a contestant dropped her bean en route, she automatically dropped out and the next player in line carried on.

For another very active game Nancy chose the Bee and the Flower. All the girls with the exception of one lined up in single file, each one holding on to the waist of the person in front of her. The remaining girl became a sunflower. The object of the game was for the entire line of bees to ensnare the "flower." To catch the flower, the head and tail of the line must surround the flower and enclose her in the circle. This game was so much fun it was repeated several times with a different flower each time.

After all this excitement the girls were ready for a bit of handwork. Nancy showed her guests a bowl of lovely pink carnations, and asked if they would like to make some. The girls were enthusiastic. Whereupon Nancy produced the "makings" — four rolls of toilet paper — two shades of pink, one of white, and one of yellow. The toilet paper was of the double thickness variety such as Doeskin, Charmin, etc. She also brought out some wire for stems, plastic calyxes, paper carnation leaves and a roll of green tape to wrap the stems. All of the above items except the toilet tissue Nancy had bought at the dime store. Most florists also carry these items.

Then Nancy gave directions for making the natural-looking carnations. She explained, tear off three pieces of toilet tissue two sheets long. Lay them flat one on top of the other. (Counting the double sheets as two you will now have six thicknesses of paper.) Starting at one end accordion pleat the paper. Pinch it together firmly in the center and fasten it securely with one end of the stem wire. While the paper is still in folds, round off each end and cut tiny slashes across the scallops to give the ragged effect of carnation petals. Then gently separate each sheet of paper.

Slip a plastic calyx onto the wire stem up next to the flower head. Then wrap the stem with the green tape. About two inches down the wire stem wrap in two paper leaves. Add a second pair further down the stem. Draw the leaf over the dull side of a paring knife until it curls like a carnation leaf.

The girls were delighted with the results of their efforts. Each girl had her own carnation to take home and the "know-how" to make a bouquet as lovely as the one on the center of Nancy's dining table.

A few feet above the dinner table Nancy had stretched two fine wires running parallel with the sides of the table. Over these wires she draped crepe-paper streamers, forming a canopy over the table.

Her menu was summer-time fare. Nut bread sandwiches, hard boiled eggs, and lemonade. Dessert was the tradional birthday cake and ice cream, only the birthday cake was decorated with tiny blue flowers made of frosting.

Nancy's guests were enthusiastic over the party and all agreed that a Flower party in the house on a cold winter day was extra super.

APRIL RAIN PARTY

April — the month of showers! Whether the rain comes pelting down in a blustery storm or whether it comes with a soft pitter patter let's have a rain party, with paper umbrellas and rain boots pinned on curtains, lamp shades or hanging from the ceilings.

Colored construction paper, cut in the form of closed umbrellas, is fine for the invitations, with the words

Rain may come and rain may go
But parties go on forever.
Come to a rain party, at my house
Friday at three P. M.

Rain or shine meet your guests at the door with a basket of paper umbrellas and rain boots. The youngster first to draw an umbrella becomes captain of the Umbrella crew, while the first to draw a rain boot is captain of the Boots.

With their badges pinned on they are automatically divided into two teams and the fun begins.

At a hint from the hostess, the guests are quick to imagine that because of so much rain the living room floor is flooded, hence the need for "stepping stones" to cross the room through the water. Give each captain two pieces of cardboard about ten inches square.

The two captains start the relay. Each one places one stone on the floor to step on with her left foot and places the second stone as far ahead as she can step easily with her right foot. Standing on her right foot, she picks up the stone under her left foot and lays it down ahead of the right foot, and so on across the room and back, laying the stepping stones as she walks. Then she hands the "stepping stones" to next in line. Twenty-five points is awarded the team finishing first. Each captain is score keeper for her side.

Did you ever play Umbrella Ball? Open a small umbrella or parasol and put it upside down in the center of the room. The smaller the umbrella the better. The girls circle around the umbrella about three feet from it. Let the captain of the winning team in the preceding game start the game off. Each girl takes a turn at tossing the ball into an open umbrella. If the ball stays in, her team wins one point. For this game it is best to use a hard ball like a golf ball, because it bounces in and out more readily. A ping pong ball or some such light ball stays put too well to make the game exciting.

For lively competition try an indoor version of the Indian hoop and pole game. Instead of a large rope hoop and long pole used by Indian children, give each team captain a ten-inch hoop cut from heavy cardboard. The captains take turns rolling the hoop across the room while the girls try to shoot a soda straw through the hoop. For this difficult game, five points should be awarded for each successful girl.

Umbrella Catch calls for quick action. The girls form a circle at least three feet from the center. One of the captains in the center holds a tall slim umbrella, wrapped tightly for carrying, like a cane.

As she lets go of the umbrella, the girl in the circle toward whom it points must jump to her feet and catch it before it hits the floor. If she catches it her side is entitled to five points while she takes her place in the center. If she misses, the captain lets the umbrella fall in another direction.

For creative fun a "Go Away Rain" dance is tops. Give each team a pair of pan covers to be used as cymbals and urge them to create the "most." The teams should be allowed about ten minutes in separate rooms for "creating."

At one of our parties one group danced a very Indian-like heel and toe dance to the accompaniment of cymbals. The other group danced to the tune of "Rain, rain go away, Come again some other day," accented by the cymbals.

After the dances award each girl a Rainbow sash. One team can have blue sashes, the other pink sashes. Cut the sashes ahead of time from colored crepe paper.

Before refreshment time ask the captains to total the scores won by each team. Then give the girls of the winning team first choice of Miniature Japanese umbrellas. The girls from the losing team can have second choice. These tiny gay-colored umbrellas make a most appropriate favor for a Rain party.

If your rain party is to celebrate a birthday, decorate the cake with candles. Otherwise, carry out the rain idea with umbrella decorations on the cake.

To accompany the cake try Black and White ice cream floats. They are "yummy."

Recipe for Black and White ice cream float.

    3 tablespoons chocolate syrup
    Milk
    1 scoop ice cream.

Put chocolate syrup in a twelve-ounce glass. Fill two-thirds full with milk. Add ice cream and stir vigorously. Fill to the top with milk. This recipe makes one serving.

SUSIE'S ROUNDUP

Susie and her crowd had outgrown the tea-party stage. They had no time for dolls and were not yet interested in boys. Like many others of her age Susie was "cowgirl crazy." All she wanted for her birthday was a "Complete cowgirl outfit, and a party."

This posed a stumper but her clever mother found a solution. Susie's house became a ranch house and Susie invited all her crowd to a roundup. Costumes which called for jeans, boots and a sombrero brought pleasure to these young fillies who were at the moment very opposed to "dressing up."

As soon as the girls arrived at Susie's, they sensed the atmosphere of ranch life. A fire roared in the fireplace. Beside it lay a huge birch log with an ax driven into it. On the other side of the fire boots were drying.

On the newel post of the stairway stood a tin bucket of water with its accompanying dipper. Paper cups were hidden back of the bucket so no one actually drank out of the dipper.

For an opener Susie passed her cowgirl hat in which she had put a number of slips each bearing the name of a horse, such as Trigger, Silver, Knight, and others. Each guest drew one, pinned it to her dress, and became owner of that particular horse.

The first game was "Ring Pan" toss. Susie put an angel-food cake tin on a bare table, the dining table can be used, and shoved it against the wall. With small pieces of adhesive tape she marked the outer ring of the pan five points and the inner ring twenty-five points. The girls used five ping-pong balls for the game. Standing at the opposite end of the table from the cake tin, the girls took turns bouncing the balls into the pan, of course always trying to bounce into the center ring. Susie acted as scorekeeper and announced the winners.

Next the cowgirls tried their skill with a rope. A small clothesline was used as a lasso. Susie's cowgirl hat was hung on the back of a dining-room chair and the girls, standing ten feet away, tried to lasso the hat off the chair back. Each girl had three tries and was awarded another try for a successful throw.

For the third game the girls clasped hands and formed a circle. Susie's hat was placed in the center on its crown. Then the girls, keeping their hands clasped, tried to pull and push each other so as to make someone knock the hat over. Each girl who bumped the hat over dropped out of the circle. The hat was righted and the game went on, until a single winner remained.

By this time the girls were ready for a quiet game. The winner of the last game started the new one. She said, "My horse is active." The next girl in the circle to her right used the same sentence adding an adjective beginning with "b." For instance, "My horse is active and bony." The third said, "My horse is active, bony, and clever." And so on around the circle. Anyone not able to think of an adjective beginning with the next letter of the alphabet dropped out of the circle.

Then followed a "Driving Race." Two groups of three girls each were selected. In each group two of the girls were chosen as horses. These two girls made a seat of their hands, each girl taking hold of her right wrist with

her left hand and taking hold of the left wrist of the
other girl with her right hand. The horses were blindfolded. The third girl was then seated on this human
chair, and all three were turned around two or three
times until the blindfolded horses lost all sense of direction. The signal to start was given and the two teams
raced across the room and back; the blindfolded horses
being guided by the girl riders who directed them. Of
course, the team getting across the room and back first
were the winners.

By this time the cowgirls were ready for a feed. The
long dining table with its red-and-white-checked cloth
was set with shiny tin cups, plates and knives; no forks or
spoons.

For once these little girls could forget their ladylike
manners. Eating creamed potatoes and a slice of meat
loaf with a knife was not too bad, but by the time they
reached the buttered peas and Jello salad they were laughing so heartily they could scarcely eat. A slice of apple
pie to be eaten with the same knife, and a tin cup of milk
completed the hilarious meal.

At the conclusion of the party the young cowgirls gave
three "yippees" for the young hostess and her clever
cowgirl party.

A PUPPET PARTY

For something new and different that will rate tops with your gradester daughter and her pals try a balloon puppet party. The only materials needed for these unusual puppets are a supply of balloons, some tempera paints, a little soap, and some pieces of gay crepe paper and bits of ribbon and string.

When the little ladies arrive tell them they can make their own puppets and a prize will be given for the cleverest, the funniest, the most unusual, and the gayest. Be sure to have plenty of table room for the girls to work on and shears handy to cut the crepe paper.

Because rubber is slick, it is best to first rub the balloons with a soapy lather. This soapy covering when dry makes the paint adhere more easily to the rubber.

Inflate the balloon before painting on the faces. Either tempera paint or ink can be used. The girls will be delighted with the expressions they have created. Tie the balloon as close up as possible leaving the neck of the balloon free.

The girls will want to design hats from the colored crepe paper. These hats can be stuck on with cellulose tape or tied on with ribbons under the chin. A chinaman's queue can be made of braided black embroidery cotton.

When the puppets are completed, each girl can fasten her creation to her finger by slipping the neck of the balloon over her finger and fastening it on with a rubber band. Now all is ready for the "Puppet Parade."

If each girl makes up a bit of the life history or perhaps a spicy romance concerning her puppet, it adds to the fun. She can introduce her puppet to the rest of the guests, giving the puppet's name, telling who he is, and what he's famous for. For instance, a Chinaman puppet might be the best laundryman in town; another wearing a George Washington paper hat might be a statesman; another wearing a cap with a small visor could be a bellhop at the leading hotel. The possibilities for a lot of imaginative fun are limitless.

Convert a handy table into bleachers for the puppet audience while the girls entertain with some stunts, for by now the lassies will be ready for some active games.

Divide the girls into two teams for a "Paper Relay." Give the first player of each team two pieces of cardboard about eight by ten inches. The player steps on one piece of cardboard with her left foot and places the other piece as far ahead as she can easily step with her right foot. Standing on her right foot, she picks up the cardboard from under her left foot and advances it ahead of the right foot. The object of the game is to walk across the room and back, stepping on the paper all the way. In other words, the player lays her own stepping stones as she goes. This game is hilariously funny and exciting as a relay. The team finishing first is of course the winner.

For the next bit of excitement line the girls up in two straight rows facing each other. Draw a chalk line in front of their toes (chalk will vacuum off the rug with no trouble). Give each girl a piece of the cardboard that was used in the last game, but this time to be used as a fan.

Toss two ping-pong balls between the two rows of girls. The object of the game is for each team to fan the ball over the opponents' line. The girls must stay behind the lines. The balls can't be touched—only fanned. A referee keeps track of the score and announces the winners. The action of these elusive little balls makes this a really exciting game.

Another circle game girls of this age will enjoy is called "Jingle Bell." The girls stand in a circle with their hands behind them. One player is given the bell. A leader is chosen to stand in the center of the circle and close her eyes. She then counts slowly to ten, the counts coming about a second apart. Upon the first count, whoever has the bell rings it vigorously and then takes the clapper in her hand and passes it behind her back to her neighbor either to the right or left. On the count of ten, the movements stop and the leader opens her eyes. She guesses who has the bell. Anyone caught with the bell becomes the next leader.

By this time the girls will be ready for refreshments. To carry out the puppet idea serve a puppet meal. Arrange on each plate a complete doll. The head is half a hard-boiled egg with raisin eyes, nose and mouth—shredded yellow cheese for hair—a peach pickle body with raisin buttons—celery arms—and a lettuce leaf for a skirt. Under the lettuce leaf will be a generous serving of your favorite hot dish—macaroni and cheese, or tuna, or creamed chicken. The girls will be delighted with these tasty attractive puppets. Ice cream is always an acceptable dessert to the young fry.

Each guest will be anxious to take her puppet balloon home to show her family and will rate this party as tops.

A DOGGY AFFAIR

Most youngsters love dogs and Joan and her crowd were no exception. For that reason she decided to make her birthday party a "Doggy Affair." When she invited her friends she asked each of them to bring a snapshot of her dog and be prepared to give a two-minute talk on the virtues of that particular breed of dog. Immediately the gang was interested.

As each guest arrived Joan handed her an envelope which contained paper letters. These letters when placed in the right order spelled out a dog's name such as Rover, Brownie, Scotch, Lassie, etc. This is an excellent starter as it gives each newcomer something to do while the others are arriving. As soon as each one had figured out her dog's name it was written on a slip of paper and pinned on her and became her name for the evening. One plump gal turned out to be "Lassie," and the sober scholar of the bunch became "Soot," much to the crowd's delight.

The first activity of the evening was a "Handful Relay." The girls were divided into two teams. Fifteen dog biscuits were given to the first player in each team. At a signal she put all of them on the floor in front of the person next to her in line. Each player had to have all the dog biscuits in her hands when she passed them. If a player

48

spilled some of them in the passing, the line started over again. The team that finished first won the relay.

Next Joan passed a hat containing slips of paper. Each guest drew one. On each slip was written a situation to be acted out by the person drawing it in bow-wow language only. Here are some good situations:

Bing Crosby singing a sentimental ballad.

A bashful boy explaining to teacher why he was late to school.

A boy teasing to play out after dark with the crowd.

A mother scolding her small son for breaking a window.

A father refusing to increase his son's allowance.

The trick was to guess what situation was being portrayed by the person barking through her assignment. The one doing the best job of explaining her situation in dog language was given a bag of dog biscuits.

The following game took a great deal of wind. The players stood in two lines. At the head of each line was placed a stack of No. 2 paper sacks; one for each player. At a given signal the first person in each line picked up a bag, ran to the end of her line, blowing it up as she ran and popped it on the back of the end girl as she stepped into line behind her. If the bag failed to burst, she blew it up and tried again. As soon as the explosion was heard the second person in line took her turn with a sack. The side finishing first won a picture of a dog clipped from a magazine cover.

After this hilarious game the girls needed a bit of time to catch a breath, so they played Dark Dog. Each girl was given a 4 x 6 blank card and a pencil. The players were warned to take a good look at the card because they were going to be blindfolded. When all were blindfolded they were asked to draw a dog. After this they were told to put a collar on the dog. Then to draw a bone in front of him.

And then to draw a license tag hanging from his collar. The blindfolds were then removed and the astounding pictures exhibited.

While lunch was being prepared girls displayed the snapshots of their pet dogs, and gave the two-minute talks they had prepared about their dogs and the advantages of that particular breed.

Refreshments for Joan's party were simple. Hot dogs, and milk, with frozen ice-cream dogs for dessert were served from a table covered with a gay-colored paper tablecloth which was decorated with dog cut-outs. A cardboard doghouse was the centerpiece. Favors were small figures of dogs.

Joan and her crowd voted this Doggy affair tops among their party experiences.

A NUTTY PARTY

"Can't I ever have a party unless it's my birth-day?" Sally demanded.

Her mother looked up from her mending star-tled. "Why, I hadn't thought of it that way, Sally. I just took it for granted that children's parties meant a birth-day party."

"You and Daddy have more parties than just one a year," answered Sally. "I don't see why I can't."

Sally's mother thoughtfully considered the question. Why shouldn't a youngster entertain her friends at least as often as her parents entertain theirs. Then she replied. "I think, Sally, that you have a point. If you would like to entertain your friends, of course you can have a party."

So Sally and her mother sat down together to plan a party. Sally suggested that since this was sort of a nutty idea of hers why not make it a nutty party. Why not in-deed?

The invitations were typed on slips of thin paper which read:

You are invited to a Nutty Party, Friday after school, February 4, at the Nut House, 805 Blunt Street. Wear a Nutty costume for a Nutty good time (Signed) Your Nutty friend, Sally.

These invitations were then folded small enough to fit English walnut shells which Sally delivered to the girls she wanted at her party.

Friday afternoon arrived and so did the guests, one dressed in Mother's long dress, one wearing a big hat and long earrings, and others in whatever strange apparel appealed to them as a Nutty Costume.

Sally met the girls at the door with a nut basket containing green and white badges about the size and shape of a big walnut shell. Each shell bore the name of a nut such as Wal, Hickory, Beech, Pecan, Hazel, Butter, Brazil, Cashew, Filbert, and Chest. The girl drawing the first green shell became the Head Nut for the Greens—the first girl taking a white shell became Head Nut for the Whites. The girls then pinned the nutty names on themselves and answered to those names for the evening. Of course Chest and Butter came in for quite a ribbing.

Even girls like to use their muscles now and then and show their strength, so for a Relay scaled to her living room Sally had a contest to discover the nuttiest team. She stretched a piece of tape about eight feet long on the floor. First the Head Nuts from each team stood on the line facing each other. Each girl stood with both feet on the line, with heel and toe touching the line. Each contestant clasped the right hand of her opponent. Then by pulling, each tried to make the other player lose her balance without losing her own. The one who stepped off the line first lost a point. The one who stayed on the line won a point for her team. If both stepped off at the same time they started over again. They continued this relay until each girl had a turn. Then the Head Nuts added up the points and announced the winning team.

Next Sally had a "Living Room Balloon Race." The girls of each team sat in a row on the floor, one directly back of the other, so that the two teams made two parallel rows. The Greens were handed a green balloon and the Whites a white one. At a signal the Head Nut in each row passed the balloon from the palm of her right hand to the palm of the right hand of the person behind her, who in turn followed suit—and so on down the line. The last girl transferred the balloon to her left hand and passed it up the line again, this time by the left hand. At no time could the player touch the balloon with her free hand. If it fell off, the player behind picked it up with both hands and passed it on with one hand. The first team to return the balloon to the Head Nut won and was awarded twenty-five points.

Another active living-room game that was nutty enough to suit the girls was called "True or False." The girls gathered in the center of the living room and were told the West end of the room was the False end and the East end the True. Sally read a list of statements which she had prepared beforehand about nut subjects. For instance, the leader read, "The peanut is a nut that grows above ground." The first girls at the head of each line answered by going to the False corner of the room, which in this case was correct. Therefore, each girl won a point for her side. The second girls in each line answered the next question—and so on to the end of the lines. Other nutty statements were:

> The beechnut grows on the beach by the sea.
> The hazelnut is a female nut.
> The walnut is common in Minnesota.
> The hickory nut grows on a tree famous for its wood.
> The butternut comes from cows.
> The chestnut is common around Christmas time.

To occupy the girls while their lunch was being prepared Sally started them on "Fortune Telling" peanuts.

Sally had removed the peanuts from their shells ahead of time. Into the shells she put tiny folded bits of paper on which were written such words as "journey," "wealth," "success," "5 children," "2 husbands," and "hard work." These she had hidden around the room. The girls were told that somewhere in the room was a peanut with her fortune inside. Each girl must hunt until she found one. After everyone had a peanut they opened up the shells and took turns reading the fortunes they found. Providing only one apiece eliminated that scramble that usually accompanies an indoor hunt.

These are some of the games that kept Sally and her friends busy at her Nutty Party. At the close of the fun the Head Nut of each team added up the scores each team had won, and the winning team was then given the privilege of having the losers serve them lunch. Sally lighted a fire in the fireplace and the girls squatted around on the floor to eat hot dogs and buns and drink pop. When the winners were all supplied with food the losers then received their hot dogs and sat by the fire to tell tall tales as they ate.

After the party Sally said, "Gee, Mom, that was a swell party."

Sally's mother was glad she had permitted Sally to have the party not only because Sally and her friends had such a good time, but she realized that Sally had learned a great deal about being a good hostess. Sally had made an effort to bring the shy girl into the games and had learned the value of cooperating with a hostess—valuable knowledge that will help Sally enter adolescence with more poise and ease.

A "JEAN" PARTY

There's a bit of tomboy in every lass that bubbles with joy at the suggestion of a "Jean" party. In our neighborhood jean parties are the popular Friday night entertainment for the eleven-to-thirteen-year-old girls. Kristen's party was typical.

Kristen invited her crowd for supper, and for the jean crowd, believe it or not, that means wieners and buns, potato chips, dill pickles, baked beans and spaghetti; favorite dishes of the jeanites. As Kristen's mother said, "Those youngsters would eat that food every night, if they were at a party."

If the moon is bright, Kristen says, the crowd likes nothing better than an old-fashioned game of "Hide and Seek." Just in case some of the girls might be inclined to wander too far away, thereby getting out of hand, there are strict rules requiring the girls to hide only in and around Kristen's yard.

For the ordinary get-together party nothing is considered more fun than quizzes and guessing contests. One of the popular games is "Guess It." Divide the girls into teams of four and seat them around a card table. The leader of each team leaves the room with the hostess. The leaders are told to return to their tables and draw something. It may be a picture of Betsy Ross at work on the first flag or any other subject the leaders may decide upon. If the leaders have no artistic ability so much the funnier. The object of the game is for the girls at each table to guess just what it is their leader is drawing. The table finishing first is the winner.

Another popular stunt at Kristen's party was a musical spell down. The girls divided into two groups and stood facing each other. Kristen acted as pronouncer by playing snatches of tunes at the piano. If the first girl at the head of the line could not name the tune being played she sat down. Then the girl at the head of the line opposite took her chance, and so on down the two lines. The last one to stand was the winner.

"Jay-walking" is a good jean-party game. The girls line up in two teams of equal numbers and the first one on each team is given a cane (a yardstick will do). She rests her forehead on her hands on the cane handle, keeps her eyes on the floor, while she circles the cane six times. When she finishes the sixth round she walks to the opposite end of the room, touches a designated spot on the wall, then goes back to the starting point and yields the cane to the next contestant in line. This doesn't sound exciting, but the dizzy stagger of the contestants is very funny. Each contestant is sure he can do it without staggering.

The jean crowd likes animals. They also love quiz games, so here is one especially suitable. Give each girl a pencil and a paper prepared beforehand with a list of animals, fowl, or what-have-you, and with the words "male, female, and offspring" opposite each name. Here is Kristen's list that can be used, or another may be substituted.

	Male	*Female*	*Offspring*
Deer	Buck	Doe	Fawn
Goat	Billy	Nanny	Kid
Dog	Dog	Bitch	Pup
Donkey	Jack	Jenny	Foal

	Male	Female	Offspring
Fox	Dog	Fox	Vixen
Hog	Boar	Sow	Shoat
Seal	Bull	Cow	Calf
Goose	Gander	Goose	Gosling
Duck	Drake	Duck	Duckling

This game proves to be quite a challenge.

Another popular quiz with the jeanites is called "Human Traits." Kristen gave each of her guests a sheet of paper and pencil and then asked them to write as many words as they could which describe the characteristics of teen-agers. Some of the jeanites immediately listed all the good characteristics like honesty, sincerity, and beauty. Others tried to make up a gruesome list. Anyway it was lots of fun and at the end of fifteen minutes the one with the longest list was declared winner.

After this mental effort the girls were more than ready to use their heads in another fashion. They formed a circle and each was given a book. Each girl balanced her book on her head and marched to music. When the music stopped each girl knelt on the floor and remained in that position until the music began again. If the book fell to the floor or was touched by the hand of the player, that player was disqualified and withdrew. The game continued until only one player was left.

After a bit of discussion on this and that, the girls scattered to their homes with words of appreciation for the nice party—one of many enjoyed by Kristen and her crowd.

For Sturdy Lads

A PARTY FOR YOUNG
CARPENTERS

Tommy wanted a birthday party. In fact he insisted upon it. Naturally we hesitated. It would take some doing, we reasoned, to entertain a bunch of wrestling, scrapping, shoving young eight-year-olds.

Nevertheless a birthday can't be ignored. Nothing to do but settle down with young Tom and plan a party.

Tommy, screwing his face into a thoughtful frown, said, "I wish we could build something. All the guys like to saw and pound." That was the springboard of our idea. A bright cardinal whistling from our neighbor's feeding tray gave us the next thought. A bird-feeding tray wouldn't be too hard for an eight-year-old to make and there would be just about time enough after school for each boy to make one. That suited Tommy.

First came the invitations. They read:

A carpenter's party at
Tommy Durand's house,
Friday after school.

We printed them on pieces of shingle four inches long and one inch wide. On the reverse side of the shingle went the guest's name. Tommy delivered these invita-

60

tions to his guests the following day. Needless to say, the boys were immediately interested.

Next came getting material for the trays. The wood must be soft enough to be easily handled. Wooden fruit boxes from the neighboring store are just the thing. The store was glad to get rid of them as it saved hauling them away.

Tommy's Dad collected an adequate supply of orange crates, narrow-stripped cantaloupe boxes, and sturdy apple boxes. Tommy and his Daddy took the crates apart and piled the boards neatly into a miniature lumber yard at one end of the basement. From friends we borrowed enough additional saws and hammers to provide for each guest. These were arranged in a neat row on Tom's work bench.

Even though the work bench is a large one we felt that if eight young sprouts hammered and sawed at the one bench it was likely to result in pounded fingers and ruffled tempers. Therefore we arranged solid wooden apple boxes in a circle around the work bench, thus providing each boy with a place to work.

When Friday came the boys were right on hand after school. Each boy was given a boy-size carpenter's apron with a supply of shingle nails in the pocket. Each apron was made of sturdy material and was about eighteen inches long and twelve inches wide. A crosspiece was stitched on the lower half of the apron and up through the center to form two pockets. Sturdy tape was sewed to the top for a halter and the same tape was used for the apron strings. Every boy has seen carpenters wear such aprons, and each was delighted to have one of his very own.

We showed the boys the feeding tray next door thinking they might like to follow its pattern. We told them they were to take home their finished trays. One practical

lad immediately asked, "Where'll we get the lumber?"
And we answered, "You'll find lumber and tools in the
basement."

The boys tore through the house like a thundering
herd and down into the basement. In no time at all each
boy was choosing from the little lumberyard the boards
with which he wanted to work. In a shorter time than it
takes to tell, each boy was busy making a tray of his own
design.

The saws hummed and the hammers pounded as the
happy voices of the youngsters compared notes on their
progress.

Near the end of the afternoon we inquired if they were
ready to eat. For the first time in our experience with
boys at parties we were greeted with "Can't we have just
a little more time? We aren't quite through."

At last all were ready to eat. To each one we handed
a workman's box lunch. The boys were excited over this
new version of a birthday party lunch. Each box contained peanut butter and lettuce sandwiches, a half pint
bottle of milk and a straw, an apple, a piece of birthday
cake and a sucker.

After lunch the trays were brought up for display. Not
one of the young carpenters had copied the neighbor's
tray but each had followed his own design. They were all
very clever. One was simply a tray with an edge around it
to prevent food from falling off. Another was a bird house
with a tray porch while still another had a broad peaked
roof.

On leaving the party each guest was presented with a
package of bird seed from the dime store. While the boys
were collecting their trays, bird seed and carpenter's
aprons to take home, one enthusiastic lad said, "This is
the best party I've been to in three years." A little tousle-
head replied, "What d'ya mean—three years—it's the most

fun of them all." Then we knew that our carpenter workshop idea had made a hit.

If your noisy lad wants the gang in for a party don't hesitate to give the go-ahead signal. For a party that's fun, economical and easy to manage try the carpenter workshop idea—it really works.

A KITE PARTY

"Gee Mom, March is a punk month for a birthday. You can't have a sleigh ride because the snow's gone. You can't have a picnic 'cause it's too cold. I wish my birthday came some other month."

Nine-year-old Chuck pressed his snub nose against the windowpane as he looked out at the bleak day. "If it were near the end of March maybe the weather would be halfway decent—but March 6th—that's awful."

"We can always have an indoor party and play games, Chuck," I suggested brightly.

"Yeah we've done that at every birthday party all winter. The fellows are all tired of that."

"There must be something we can do for the boys on your birthday that would be fun." We both looked out at the tree tops bending low in the strong March wind.

I had a thought. It'll soon be kite time. "Chuck, why not have a kite party?"

Chuck looked up with a pleased grin. "A kite party! What'd you know? Well—it's different anyway. What's the idea?"

That was the beginning of Chuck's kite party given in the blustery month of March, when it's too raw and disagreeable to give a party outside and yet not wintry enough for a skating or sleigh-ride party.

"First come the invitations. Let's have them different

too." Chuck had forgotten his disgust and the plans were on.

From the dime store we bought white cards three by five inches and cut them kite-shaped. The invitations read:

> Kite time is here. Come to Chuck's party Friday night
> after school.

An address and stamp on the reverse side and the invitations were ready for the mail. Curiosity ran high with the crowd. What was going to happen? This sounds like fun.

Ahead of party time Chuck bought a supply of balsam wood from which he cut thin strips to be used for the frames. Then we laid in a supply of bright-colored crepe paper, a jar of paste and plenty of strong string. We were all set for the excited crowd that arrived breathlessly after school. On birthday party nights boys always run all the way from school to get to the party quickly. No time to waste when a party is on.

As soon as the boys had gathered Chuck showed his guests a kite he had made as an experiment and then told the boys if they would like to build kites the "makings" were in the basement. In less time than it takes to tell the crowd was downstairs looking over the material, fingering the saws and setting up shop on a sturdy apple crate.

We have long since learned that where many boys are working with tools it is better to have saws and hammers for each. We had supplemented our own supply by borrowing from our friends. So that each boy would have a place to work without interference we had put in a supply of strong apple boxes from the corner grocery. These make excellent individual work benches.

For a small outlay kites all ready to assemble can be

bought at the dime store, but Chuck felt the boys would enjoy making their own.

The kites are really simple to make. The frame is made with two or three sticks to form a cross, or an X with a crosspiece. Tiny nails from cigar boxes can be used to nail the sticks in the form wished.

By cutting a groove in the ends of the sticks, a strong string can be strung from stick to stick forming the frame on which to stick the paper.

The kite frame may then be covered with common tissue paper, light-weight wrapping paper, or even newspaper. We chose crepe paper because of its decorative value. It is a little harder to paste, but kites covered with crepe paper fly very smoothly.

When each boy had completed the body of his kite the tail came in for consideration. Because the tail must be as light as possible to avoid weighing down the kite, we tied small pieces of paper about a foot apart on a long light string. The small pieces of paper are loosely rolled, then tied in the middle like a bow.

Before too long the boys had finished their kites. While they were waiting for the paste to dry we called the boys up to the kitchen for refreshments. To keep in the groove with boy taste we served the traditional hamburgers and buns, with brimming cups of hot chocolate in which floated a marshmallow. The birthday cake dessert was decorated with nine small kites of frosting with a candle in the center of each.

Lunch over, the boys went to the school ground to test-fly their masterpieces. Before they left the house we gave each a card on which we had typed the following safety rules for good kite fliers. These rules are issued by the Safety Service of Electrical Companies throughout the country, and the National Safety Company.

A good kite flier does not fly his kite near electric telephone or trolley wires, or near high voltage trans-
mission towers.

He does not use wire or tinsel twine of any sort or
even a wet string.

He does not fly his kite in a thunderstorm.

He does not use a kite with metal ribs.

He does not run across highways, but flies his kite in
open places away from traffic.

At dusk Chuck's father rounded up the gang of happy
kite fliers and took them home. Each boy declared he
enjoyed making his own kite and was pleased to have it
for future flying days. The boys voted Chuck's party "a
high-flier of a birthday party."

"NO SISSY GAMES"

"Take a tip from me," warned my friend, "and never, never give a party for a bunch of ten-year-old boys. After Hugh's last party it took a week to clean up the wreckage."

I quaked in my boots at her warning because I had already promised our rough-and-tumble Sandy a party. What to do! I didn't want to back out, for if Sandy was ever to become a gracious host now was the time to start. We all realize that social ease can't be put on like a new coat at a certain age, but is acquired by practice and usage as a youngster develops.

So Sandy and I sat down at the kitchen table to plan his party. "We don't want any sissy games, Mother," said Sandy running his fingers through his mop of curly red hair. "The fellows like things lively."

I suppressed a shudder—we have no amusement room and "lively" games for a dozen active ten-year-olds didn't sound too promising for our living-room furniture. But the party must go on. So after much discussion pro and con—I supplied most of the cons—we settled on a "G-man" party.

Then came the search for games—games tailored to our chosen theme; games boisterous enough to suit Sandy and his friends and at the same time leave the living room in good shape for future use.

Since ten-year-olds get an extra thrill from an evening party, an evening party this must be from seven to nine o'clock. Two hours for which to plan entertainment. Allowing twenty minutes for refreshments—a ten-year-old can do pretty well for himself in that time—we would still have an hour and forty minutes for games. We have learned from experience that about seven minutes is a good average for a game. Therefore we needed fifteen games to fill out the evening.

When we had decided on our games we gathered all the necessary props. We then pasted a list of the games to the inside of a kitchen cupboard door where they could be referred to quickly to avoid delay between games. For we have learned—the hard way—that a few idle moments is apt to result in a wrestling match which can quickly develop into a free-for-all.

On the night of the party promptly at seven the guests, cowlicks slicked down and shirts stuck in, arrived. Our well-scrubbed Sandy met them at the door with a hat full of small red stars and green paper shields. The red stars bore the letters F.B.I. The green shields a big T. This drawing automatically divided our "G-men" into two camps. The first boy to draw a star became the F.B.I. captain. The first boy to draw a shield became "T" captain.

Sandy announced that the F.B.I. men would compete with the "T" men in games. Points would be given the winners. Sandy asked each captain to appoint a scorekeeper for his team. He announced that the side with the most points at the close of the evening would be served refreshments by the losers.

The first competition was a "Footprint Relay" race scaled to fit our living room. Boy-sized paper footprints marked two circles around the room, one for each team. To make the footprints we had traced around the sole of

Sandy's shoe on white wrapping paper. When cut out these were surprisingly good. Then we scotch-taped them to the carpet at various angles. Each boy had to fit his foot exactly to each print. Each boy completing the circle started the next boy in line on his team by touching him. The team that finished first was awarded ten points.

To find out which team was the stronger we conducted tournament style a bottle wrestle. We put six empty milk bottles around the room with plenty of space between. Then each F.B.I. man chose a "T" man opponent as nearly his own size as possible. With the bottle on the floor between them they faced each other and placed hands on partner's shoulders. The object of the game was to see which man could pull or push his partner until he forced him to bump over the bottle. The one who bumped over the bottle was the loser, of course. All of the winners then played each other until there was only one winner left. The winner was awarded twenty-five points for his team. For evenly matched boys this proves a very strenuous game, takes very little room and is not as rough-house as it sounds. But it will completely wind the most active youngster.

To give the boys a chance to catch their breath we next had fingerprint fortunes. Beforehand we had written some fortunes on pieces of white paper with secret ink. To do this we dissolved one tablespoonful of common table salt in one half cup of water and wrote with a clean stub point pen. In writing with secret ink dip the pen frequently. Then before the writing dries draw a black pencil line under the fortune to indicate the location of the sentence on the paper. Let the writing thoroughly dry before laying the papers together.

Sandy handed these apparently blank sheets of paper to the "G" men who were told to press their thumbs on an ink pad and then on the paper. Thus they fingerprinted their own fortunes. Sandy then told the boys that five points would be awarded the team that first discovered their own fortunes. Each boy was given a soft lead pencil. They soon found that words would appear by rubbing the pencil lightly over the paper. Here are some of the fortunes we used, geared strictly to boy humor.

1. Don't get killed in the dark of the moon——it's fatal.
2. You'll soon be dead——dead wrong.
3. Don't watch the clock so much——it may strike.
4. It's unlucky for you to drown on Friday the 13th.
5. Don't cultivate a taking way——your friends may miss things.
6. Your rich relatives will soon leave you——but they won't leave you much.
7. If you're searching for clue, look under "c" in the dictionary.
8. Never take a job on the 32nd day of the month.

For the next contest the F.B.I. men lined up on one side of the room and the "T" men on the other. The captain of each team was presented with an ordinary pasteboard fan. In front of each team was laid a small tissue-paper fish marked "clue." These detectives were told to fan their clues to the opposite end of the room and back—then to pass the fan to the next man on their team. If you've ever tried this stunt you'll see why the boys enjoyed it so much. The first team to finish was given twenty-five points.

These were the games that delighted Sandy and his crowd right up to refreshment time. At the close of the evening the scores were added and the losing team took their places behind the dining-room table which was covered with a paper tablecloth. The losing F.B.I. men then donned aprons and served "hot dogs" and buns to the winning "T" team. The "T" men were very demanding that the losers doctor the wieners with just the right amount of mustard and piccalilli. After the winners were filled up, a fresh supply was brought on for the losers.

The only trouble with this party was the difficulty in getting the lads to go home on time. Each one had a stunt that he wanted to show the fellows. We really knew that Sandy and his guests had a rousing good time, and not a bit of damage was done to the living-room furnishings. I'll admit the boys kicked up some dust and made a lot of noise, but after all this was a boys' party and we all enjoyed their harmless hilarity.

THE FELLOWS LIKE THINGS
A BIT ROUGH!

"Be sure to have some boisterous games, Mom. The fellows like things a bit rough, you know."

That was our ten-year-old's comment as we sat down together to plan a party.

My heart did a flip-flop because we have no amusement room and "boisterous" games for a bunch of ten- and eleven-year-olds sound like a bad omen for the living-room furnishings. However, we didn't refuse because we genuinely wanted to welcome Tom's friends to our home.

Because all boys at one time or another dream of life on the wide open ranges, we decided this would be a cowboy party. For invitations Tom gathered some birch bark and on it printed in black ink the following:

All cowhands are invited to the Bar-B Ranch on Friday night next at 7 P.M.   Tom.

The invitations set tongues awaggin'. All the boys came on time—cowboy outfits complete even down to the six-shooters. As the guests arrived Tom gave each lad a brand to wear for the evening—half were Bar-B and the other half QT ranchers. All guns were checked at the door, because as Tom said this was no shootin' fray.

As soon as the lads had all got there, Tom asked the boys from the two ranches to line up in two separate lines for a "Bundle Relay." Then he gave the first player in each line a ball of cord. When the signal was given each leader passed the ball to the next boy in line but held on to the end of the string. As the balls passed down the lines the cord unwound. When the end of the line was reached the balls in each line were passed up the lines behind the backs of the players until they reached the first players again. The object was to see which team could first wrap itself into a bundle.

The sequel to the race consisted in untying the bundle by passing the balls back and winding the cord as it went.

Next was a circle game with one of the QT ranch hands on the outside of the circle. He tapped one of the Bar-B hands on the back and said, "Good Morning." The Bar-B boy answered, "Good Morning." The QT lad said, "Have you seen my calf?" The Bar-B boy asked, "How is it dressed?" The QT rancher then described a boy in the circle. As soon as the "calf" recognized himself or the Bar-B boy knew who was being described, both began to run outside the circle, the Bar-B boy trying to catch the calf before it got back to its place in the circle. When this happened the calf had to go into the center of the circle, which was the corral, where he remained until the end of the game. Whether or not the calf was caught, the Bar-B rancher became the next questioner outside the circle. The questioner did not chase. When he had described his calf he stepped into the place left by the Bar-B rancher whom he had just questioned. There was no escape from the corral. Players who were caught remained in the center until the end of the game.

Good cowhands must be good horsemen and have good balance. Lacking horses at this party, Tom substituted a broomstick balance. A bridge was made by laying a broomstick on the seats of two chairs a slight distance apart. With the aid of a cane the contestant seated himself on the broomstick and crossed his legs. When he was nicely balanced he endeavored to remove with his cane two handkerchiefs that were hung on the back of the chair behind him. Three falls were allowed before he was declared a loser.

The hands from the two ranches took turns trying this balance game. The ranch with the most winners of course won the relay.

"Fetch and Carry" was a bit different in the way of relays. Two players, the first and second, in each team joined hands. When Tom said, "Go!" they ran to the goal line across the room. The first remained there while the second hurried back and joined hands with the third player. These two ran to the goal, and the second player remained while the third returned for the fourth. The ranch that first transferred all its members to the goal line won the race.

Boys always like to test their muscles, so we chose "Hand Push" for a living-room challenge. Two boys, from the two ranches, stood facing each other with their toes touching. They had their palms also touching on a level with their chests. In this position each pushed the other's hands until one was forced to step back. The player who forced his opponent backward was the winner. As soon as the boys saw this game, nothing would do but all must try it.

For refreshments Tom led his ranchers into the big kitchen where his mother had set out a hearty lunch for hungry cowhands. The only light in the room was furnished by a flickering barn lantern set in the middle of the table.

The dishes were tin, the table was bare. The fare was simple but hearty and, followed by strawberry shortcake and tall glasses of milk, satisfied even the hungriest rancher. By curfew time, the lads picked up their guns and bade Tom a hearty good night with a "Thank you for lots of fun."

COME ON OVER, FELLOWS

"You're a glutton for punishment. I wouldn't have a bunch of ten-year-old boys in my house for a party again for anything. The last time that crowd was over here it took a week to repair the damage."

Such were the opinions expressed by the mothers of my ten-year-old son's friends, when I said that my Dick wanted to give a party.

The general opinion seemed to be that the boys could get along very nicely without parties until they reached an age when a general wrestling match was not of such paramount importance in their scheme of things. But how are these youngsters ever going to acquire any of the social graces if they have no chance to practice during their formative years?

With this thought in mind we were more than happy to allow Dick to entertain as many of his friends at a party as he wished, and thereby learn as much about being a host as he could.

Dick telephoned his invitations, "I'm having a few of the fellows over Friday night from seven to nine for an evening of fun. I'd like to have you come over." The boys accepted. An evening party; what a lark!

Next Dick and I went over the plans for the evening. As we have no amusement room the games could not be too wild and still they must be wild enough to satisfy the most active. And husky ten-year-olds are plenty active. Some of the games that I would have chosen Dick vetoed as "sissy." Occasionally we suggested a milder version of Dick's idea but eventually we worked out an evening's program.

We had two hours of entertainment for which to plan. Refreshments, of course, would take a while. Dick thought fifteen minutes would be long enough for eating and I thought a half hour. We compromised on twenty minutes, and because our refreshments were light that was about the correct time. That left one hour and forty minutes for games. From past experience with boys' parties (we're blessed with a family of sons) we have learned that the time consumed by the average game is seven minutes. Of course some games take longer and others only a few minutes but seven minutes is a good average.

Soon we had a list of fifteen suitable games. Then we went over each game and gathered together any necessary "props" that might be needed so as to avoid any delay between games.

The guests arrived promptly at seven P.M. No group of adults ever gathered so promptly at an hour set. We divided the boys up into two teams of five each and told them to see which side could make the most money first.

The leader of each row was given an empty quart milk bottle and a tablespoon. In front of each leader, placed on the buffet or a stand before a mirror, was a dish of popcorn (unbuttered and unsalted). The object is to hold the bottle, top up, on the head and, while looking into the mirror, spoon as many kernels of popcorn into the bottle as possible in three tries.

The row finishing first was given a paper on which to dump all the corn accumulated in the bottle, each kernel counting $1000. As soon as the other row finished they too counted their money. It was soon discovered that the row finishing first did not make the most money. The row finishing last' had the most corn in the bottle. This game took more than seven minutes, of course, but the next took less.

Dick asked the boys if any of them had ever seen an "Indian Wedding." He said he had heard about one and told the boys to stand in a row, facing front, shoulders touching and he'd explain how it was done. The steps of the game are:

1. The ten boys stand shoulder to shoulder, facing the front.
2. All raise hands above the head.
3. Bend to kneeling position, keeping the knees tight together.
4. Put hands behind back and clasp firmly.
5. Bend over and put forehead on the floor.

As soon as all the boys were in this position, Dick gave the lad on the end a stiff nudge, whereupon the whole group toppled over on their sides. The boys thought it great fun to have the whole row fall over. Being in kneeling position no one was hurt.

Next we had a relay called "High, Wide and Handsome." We laid newspapers on the floor a good step apart. Divided the boys into two teams of five each. Gave the leader of each team a book, told him to balance the book on his head and walk on the newspapers across the room and back. On his return the next one started. The team finishing first, of course, won the race.

Then came "Dog's Day." Ahead of time we had typed out on slips of paper, one for each lad, stunts such as these:

1. Imitate a dog meeting a cat.
2. Imitate a dog howling at the moon.
3. Imitate a dog chasing its tail, etc.

Each boy drew a slip from a hat and was warned not to let anyone see what was written on the slip. Then each fellow did as his slip directed while the rest guessed what he was doing. Some of the stunts were very amusing and some of the guesses equally so.

These were some of the games that the boys enjoyed at Dick's party. You will notice that we gave no prizes. We have found that if the games are such that everyone can participate winning seems to satisfy without a prize. Not one game called for expensive equipment. The equipment we used were things that every householder has on hand.

Although we had fifteen games planned we used only fourteen. Dick and his guests had a rousing good time and not one bit of damage was done to the household furnishings.

PARTY
IN OUTER SPACE

If your son's birthday comes in February —
that blustery month that nips noses, pinches
fingers, and storms on the day of the birthday
— plan an indoor party. With careful planning there
need be no fear of the house being torn apart.

A Party In Outer Space is ideal to catch the interest
and imagination of ten-year-olds. Write the invitations
on a card cut the shape of a rocket ship to read:

Earthman Billy Olsen
invites you
to a
Space Sports Event
at his house
Friday, February 20.

Boys receiving such an invitation will immediately want
to know "What's coming off."

Any good-sized room is ideal for a party room. Push
the furniture back against the walls and label one end
of the room "Earth" — the other end "Mars." The area
in the center of the room serves as "Outer Space."

Let your son greet his guests with a box filled with a
number of oval green paper rockets, and an equal
number of round red space ships. The rockets are
labelled "Earthmen," and the Space Ships "Martians."
This automatically divides the boys into teams and
sends them to the proper planet-end of the room. Give
each lad a pin to fasten on his ship badge.

Each team elects its own captain. Each captain is given a card and a pencil to score the points won by his team.

Because all space travelers should have a good sense of balance the first game can be a balance relay. The game is for the two teams to line up at "Earth" and race on their knees to "Mars" with an orange balanced on a tablespoon. Each player who arrives successfully wins five points for his team. The team, all of whose members arrive on Mars first, wins twenty-five points. This game has all the excitement of a race without knocking over the furniture.

All space travelers must be good shots. A marble bowling game is a good test as to which team has the greater skill. Set up ten huge spikes, one inch apart with heads down in V formation. Each captain is given three large marbles. In shooting the spikes each player must keep his knuckles on a line five feet away from the nearest spike. Every nail knocked down counts one point. If all the spikes fall at one shot that scores fifteen points. Each captain reports scores for his own side. Highest team wins another twenty-five points.

Spear throwing is a must for travelers on strange planets. Each captain is given a hoop to hold — made from a wire coat hanger. Each player, armed with three soda straw "Spears," tries to throw his spears through the hoop. The Players stand about four feet from the hoop. Once again each man is given five points for his team for every straw he throws through the hoop. After each player has tried his luck the scores are totaled, and another twenty-five points is given the winning team.

By this time the space men will be ready to relax a bit. Give each guest a raw potato with about 1½ inch cut off one end. Suggest each man trace with a paring knife on the cut end of the potato, a suitable design as an insignia for his team. Each boy should be given an old newspaper on which to work. After each lad has traced the insignia of his choice on his potato, let him cut away the background about ½ inch deep around the design.

The potato designs can be painted with tempera paint. All moisture must be wiped from the design and the paint must be put on sparingly to avoid smearing. The next step is to stamp the insignia on white cards. The best single insignia wins fifteen points a side. The best over-all design wins twenty-five points per side.

One more quiet game gives the hostess time to fix lunch. In this game each lad is given a ball of stiff dough, made by mixing equal parts of salt and flour with a bit of vegetable coloring, and just enough water to make the dough pliable. The stunt is to model, from this dough, a rocket or space ship. This, like the insignia game, is very fascinating. When the modeling is finished the crafts are set aside to harden. Fifteen points are awarded for the best of each team and twenty-five points to the overall best.

At the end of the games each captain counts winning points for his side. The losers serve lunch to the winners. If the Martians win, the Earthmen serve Hamburgers on buns, tall glasses of chocolate milk, ice cream, and of course the traditional birthday cake which can be decorated with frosted oval rockets and round space ships. As soon as the Martians are all served the Earthmen will join them with their lunch.

Each guest will be proud to take home his modeled space ship and insignia as party favors. These favors are more popular than any ready-made ones.

A MAGICIAN'S PARTY!

Every boy is born with a touch of Houdini in his soul. By the time he's twelve he'd rather pull a trick on a pal, than eat—almost. Next best he likes to watch another perform tricks of magic. So when Gray and Bernie wanted to entertain their scout troop at a magician's party, we buried our misgivings and gave the go-ahead signal.

The invitations they extended over the telephone were at least unique. "Houdini's nephew will be at our house on Friday evening. Drop around. He's going to show a few clever tricks. If you know a good stunt to show him bring it along."

This was strictly a no-refusal party. Each guest accepted and arrived promptly at seven. The guests were met at the door by two young magicians—one was attired in a Prince Albert coat and silk topper—the other wore the traditional Hindu garb. A turkish towel wound around his head served as a turban and a gay bathrobe covered his regular clothes.

The first two boys to arrive were handcuffed together. Subsequent arrivals were also handcuffed in pairs. This was done by tying each end of a forty inch string to one boy's wrists. Then another string of equal length is passed between the first boy's string and his body. Then the ends of this string are tied to his partner's wrists, linking the two boys together. The couples are to separate themselves without breaking or untying the strings.

This was an intriguing game on which the boys concentrated earnestly. It was not too long until one lad stumbled onto the solution. Yielding to loud demands he explained carefully that if one of a handcuffed pair would make a loop in his string and tuck it under the string around his partner's wrist and pull it over his partner's hand, the partners could be separated without breaking or untying the strings. Of course, the strings remained tied to the wrists. The solution was so simple it was hard for some of the boys to accept it so they continued to experiment for some time.

Next on the game list was the magic stick. The young hosts explained that touching the magic stick would prevent one from walking straight across the room to pick up a book from the floor and place it on a chair standing in one corner of the room. "Oh yeah" was the skeptical response. The boys all squatted on the floor to watch the loudest skeptic make the first try.

Following directions he stood in the center of the floor, cupped his hands over the head of a cane (yardstick) and leaned his forehead on his hands. Watching the end of the cane on the floor, he circled it six times. Then he dropped the stick and reeled across the room toward the book. He zigged when he meant to zag and landed in a heap on the floor. The boys rolled on the floor in glee. Each was sure he could do it without staggering. Each boy loath to give up tried it again and again.

Next each lad was given five toothpicks. Then Bernie announced that he'd give six more to anyone who could make them into nine toothpicks. All toothpicks must be used. Before long one bright lad discovered that by laying the toothpicks so as to print the letters N I N E he had used all his toothpicks.

Then the boys asked their guests to be seated around the floor. Bernie announced that he would remove Gray's shirt *without* removing his coat. Gray took a chair and the boys eyed him closely. Gray was very properly dressed with a dress-shirt—no tie—and coat. Bernie stepped up to him saying, "I don't like the way your collar buttons." He then unbuttoned Gray's collar and a couple of buttons down the front of the shirt. Then he criticized, "These are funny cuffs." He reached down and unbuttoned Gray's cuffs. Finally he said, "I don't like the looks of your shirt at all." He firmly gripped the back of Gray's shirt collar and pulled a bit. The shirt came off without Gray's coat being even unbuttoned.

The lads were all eyes and demanded an explanation, so after due deliberation and consultation Gray and Bernie decided they'd show the boys the stunt. The secret was that Gray had let the shirt hang down his back. By buttoning the collar and a couple of buttons down the front, and buttoning the cuffs around his wrists, the shirt appeared to be on when he was wearing a coat. When Bernie unbuttoned these few buttons it was a simple matter to pull the shirt out from under Gray's coat. However, it did look very mysterious and the boys were all anxious to try the stunt.

By the time every lad had lost his shirt at least a couple of times, the boys were ready for another trick. Gray appeared with three paper rings of identical size which hung over his left arm. "These," he said, "are magic Hindu rings. As you see they are all the same size but I will cut them in such a way that one will become two rings, another will be one long ring, and the third will make two linking rings."

He then took the first ring from his arm and cut around the ring as near the center as possible. This made two complete rings: all very simple and easy to understand.

The second ring he removed from his arm and cut exactly as he did the first, but it made one long ring. The boys began to sit up and take notice.

The last ring he cut exactly in the same way as the others, but it turned out to be a ring within a ring. Immediately the boys were clamoring to be in on the knowhow, so Gray explained.

Using an ordinary funny paper so as to have bright-colored rings, he cut three strips four inches wide the full length of the longest way of the newspaper. He then pasted the two ends of one strip together the flat way—that is, when the ends were pasted together it made a plain circle or ring. This is the ring that makes two plain rings when cut.

For the second ring—the one that turns into one long ring when cut—make one turn in the paper before pasting the ends together flatwise.

For the third ring—the one that makes a ring within a ring—make a double twist in the paper before pasting together. When Gray hung these rings over his arm the twists in the paper were not noticeable.

Before the evening was over each lad present had not only tried all the stunts the boys had prepared but had shown at least a trick or two of his own.

Tales of tricks and mystery continued as the boys sat around the table consuming huge squares of gingerbread with mounds of whipped cream. On the top side of each marshmallow, dropped into a cup of hot cocoa, was a face outlined with melted chocolate. Immediately each lad named his marshmallow for his best pal; John, Tom, or what have you.

The departing boys claimed this party was "A bagful of tricks."

A PARTY FOR
BOISTEROUS BOYS

Here's a party that teen-age boys like. They like boisterous games—"not sissy-birthday-party games." By boisterous games they mean games where they can make plenty of noise and games that require lots of action. Did I hear you say you haven't a rumpus room? Neither have we, but there are some boisterous games with lots of action that can be played in the ordinary living room and still not destroy the furniture.

Perhaps you'd like to hear about some of the games the thirteeners played at our house recently. We started off with one called "Jump the Shot." It calls for action and speed and does not need too much room. Tie an old shoe on one end of a rope. The boys form a circle sufficiently large so that each one will have room to jump. The "swinger" takes his place in the center of the circle. His rope must be at least as long as the radius of the circle. He begins by swinging the weight on a short radius, paying out the rope as he increases speed, so that by the time the object at the end of the rope reaches the players in the circle, it will be in steady motion close to the floor. Each player jumps over the rope as it passes him. It is against the rules to step out of the circle to avoid jumping. When a boy misses he drops out of the game until a second boy misses. Then these two players exchange places.

Boys love this game, but it is rather strenuous and should not be played for too long a time.

By the time this game was finished there was no trace left of the "social ice" that was so apparent when the youngsters first arrived. Most of the guests were so winded they were glad to drop into chairs or on the floor for a few moment's rest.

Now the boys were ready for a relay. Don't be alarmed —relays that are fun can be done in a small space. "Necktie Relay" is a lot of fun for fellows of this age. At best they are none too good at tying neckties and in the excitement of a relay they are indeed all thumbs, which of course only adds to the merriment. The players divide into two groups of equal numbers. Each group lines up in single file. The first player in each line is given a necktie. At the starting signal he ties the necktie around the neck of the boy just behind. As soon as the four-in-hand is tied the second player unties it, turns and ties it on the third boy and so on to the end of the line. The team who finishes first wins the game. But just a note of warning— don't use Dad's best tie—such furious tying and untying is a bit hard on the ties.

The next stunt gives the young hopefuls a chance to use some lovely big words, *a la* some of the radio comedians. Each boy takes his turn in making the longest sentence he can, beginning each important word with the same letter. For instance: "So-long sister, see you soon in San Francisco, selling silly symphonies to sarcastic sobsters." It is well to give them from three to five minutes to think up their lingo, then let each take his turn to spout. Most of them after listening to Fibber McGee and some other radio comedians will have a lingo on tap to use. A prize can go to the fellow with the most words in his sentence or the most sense in his speech.

Refreshments can be simple for boys but should be

something of which they are especially fond. Ice cream and cake is always a favorite with youngsters of this age and they like plenty of it. We set up a card table across the kitchen door and used it for a counter. The fellows lined up to get their ice cream and cake, then dropped down in some convenient place to "lick the platter clean."

After refreshments we expected the young lads to take their departure, but by this time they were thoroughly warmed up and stayed to demonstrate stunt after stunt. Each one had something to show or some trick to try.

This was one party when the boys thought the fun never ran out.

A STAG FOR THE
THIRTEENERS

Have you a thirteen-year-old son who'd like to
give a party? If you have I'll wager you are quak-
ing in your boots, but there's really nothing to
fear. Parties for lads of this supposedly trying age needn't
be free-for-all wrestling matches. They actually can be
quite enjoyable for the parents as well as the boys if you
practice a little know-how.

Parties for these active youngsters must be better
planned than for any other age group. If not well planned
the boys' excessive spirits are apt to get the better of them
and the furniture suffers accordingly. We have on a number of occasions given such parties in our living room with
no more damage than a little stirred-up dust. The secret
is to have enough planned games to occupy the entire evening—not sissy games, because boys like to be active—but
games where they can move about, meet competition, and
laugh at the other fellow.

Just recently our young thirteener asked to have "the
fellows in for a stag party." A bit breath-taking at first
thought, but we soon learned that he wanted fourteen of
his classmates in for an evening party. He had ideas about
the party and we had ideas about the living-room furniture, so we sat down together and worked out a scheme of
entertainment that proved to be very successful.

We decided to have a field meet of two competitive schools. We chose red and green as school colors. For decorations we used red and green balloons. It's fun to stick balloons on the walls and ceiling for decoration. Don't be shocked—our method leaves no marks on the wallpaper or paint. By rubbing an inflated balloon lightly and quickly on a wool rug and immediately touching the rubbed surface to the wall, the balloon will stick indefinitely. In case of a boy's party it is well to have the balloons on the upper wall or ceiling as they are less handy to pop with a pin.

As soon as the boys arrived we passed a hat in which had been placed small red and green paper pennants. The red pennants were banners for the school we called "Eatmore," the green we labeled "Sowhat." This drawing automatically divided the guests evenly between "Eatmore" and "Sowhat."

The groups were then told that the Eatmore and Sowhat schools were having a field meet. Various types of activities were to be participated in at the event. Points would be given the winner of each contest. At the close of the contest the losing team would serve as waiters to feed the winning team. The boys were immensely interested and this way of dividing them into groups left no room for hurt feelings.

We then asked each group to make up a school yell for their school to encourage the contestants. The groups retired to different rooms and had a hilarious time creating their school yell. Then they chose their own cheer leader.

The first event was a discus-throwing contest. Each school group chose a lad they felt would be the best at throwing a discus. The contestants lined up and were given paper plates which they attempted with much hilarity to throw across the room. Did you ever try to throw a paper plate? Each man was given three throws, and five points were awarded the winner of each trial. The cheer leaders led the yells to support their contestants. Each team had a scorekeeper.

The next event called for great lung power. When the men with the greatest chest expansion were chosen, one from each school, goal lines and starting lines were set and each man was given a balloon—the color to represent his school. We picked the needed balloons off the wall. The rules of the game were then given. Each man got down on his hands and knees and was told to <u>blow his balloon across the room to the goal line without touching the balloon</u>. The man who blew his balloon across the goal line first received ten points.

Not to be one-sided we next held a <u>debate</u>, two men to a team. The question was "Resolved that Eatmore is a better school than Sowhat." Naturally the Eatmore boys took the affirmative and the Sowhat boys the negative. Constructive speeches lasted three minutes and rebuttal two minutes. The guests then chose the winning team and ten points were awarded the winning side.

"<u>Shot-put</u>" next took the limelight. Empty milk bottles were placed on the floor, and the contestants stood erect and <u>dropped beans into the bottle</u>. The winner, the one with the most beans in the bottle, received ten points.

"<u>Chinese Get-up</u>," played tournament style, was next. Each Eatmore boy picked an opponent from the Sowhat school group. <u>Each pair of boys sat on the floor back to back with their arms folded across their chests</u>. At a signal they all <u>tried to rise without unfolding their arms</u>. This is lots of fun and boys love it. The Eatmore winners then competed with the Sowhat winners until there was one remaining winner. If two men from the same school are winners then twenty-five points can be awarded each man.

The scores of all the games were then added up and the losing team retired to one side of the dining-room table which was covered with a paper tablecloth. A plentiful supply of hot wieners and a heaping platter of buttered buns was set before the losers, who were given aprons. The losers then served the hot dogs over the counter (dining table) to the winners. Mustard or piccalilli was served upon request. After the winners were completely filled up a fresh supply was brought for the losers.

The main difficulty with this party is getting the boys to go home at the scheduled time. Each one has a stunt he'd like to offer. When this happens you can be sure the boys have had a good time. For some time after the party, Eatmore and Sowhat were by-words with the boys.

A TEEN-AGE PARTY

A party for a bunch of thirteen-year-old boys—
I quailed at the prospect. A party for younger
boys (and there had been plenty of them at our
house) was all right and easy to manage. But thirteen!
That fussy age—too old for a small boy party and not quite
old enough for a young man party. However our thirteen-
year-old was all for giving a party for the bunch. We did
not want to refuse because we believe along with many
others that it is wise to welcome your sons' friends in the
home.

"Shall it be a dinner party or an evening party, and do
you want to invite both boys and girls?" I asked, hoping
that girls might be included for their supposedly quieting
influence on lively boys. No, this was to be a "stag" in the
evening with refreshments.

"We don't want a bunch of paper and pencil games,
Mother," he admonished. "That's too much like school."

Already I had pictured the boys quietly sitting around
card tables playing card games or doing quizzes. Quickly
I revised my thinking—this was to be an active party for
active boys. The boys, fourteen of them, were invited, and
games were planned. The evening arrived and so did the
boys. Some were dressed in suits and white shirts, others in
flannel shirts and corduroys, while several arrived dressed
as comedians. While the boys were arriving they seemed

to be a bit self-conscious. Lads at this age are not exactly social butterflies, although these boys came from homes where parties among both adults and children were frequent.

As soon as the clan had gathered and as a starter for the evening's fun we placed empty quart milk bottles (seven of them) around the room with plenty of space between. The boys were matched in pairs according to size as much as possible for the good old "bottle wrestle." Each boy places his hands on his partner's shoulders facing each other with a bottle between them. The object of the game is to push or pull your partner in such a manner that he is forced to bump over the bottle. The one who knocks the bottle down is the loser of course. All of the winners play each other, tournament fashion, until there is only one winner left. For evenly matched boys this proves a very strenuous game, takes very little room and is not as "rough-house" as it sounds.

The little "stiffness" at first apparent was entirely lost during and after this game. The fellows were so winded they subsided into chairs or on the floor for a moment's rest.

As soon as the boys had regained their breath they were ready for a relay. They divided into two teams, seven on each side. Two strips of white tape (the kind that comes in rolls for sewing) were stretched across the floor, with ends pinned to the rug. This represented two back fences. The boys became cats. The leader of each team starting at the same time, backed along the fence (tape) with both hands and feet on the tape. When they reached the other end of the fence they turned and backed again to where they had begun. As soon as the leaders were back the second ones in line started. The side finishing first won the relay. This relay is exciting, requires skill and speed, and can be harmlessly played in a small space.

Boys enjoy this next game because it not only gives them plenty of action but also calls for noises with their vocal chords. The lads were arranged in little circles of three all about the room. A chosen leader gave directions such as "traffic to the right," at which call the little circles turned to the right and kept turning until the leader said, "traffic to the left," when they quickly shifted and started turning to the left.

When the leader called, "beep beep," all the players quickly formed a new circle with two other people. As they did this they all blew their "vocal" horns. While the circles were being changed, the leader stepped in and the boy left over became the new leader. The interest in this game is increased if there is some lively music being played at the same time.

Next the boys played a "Life-Saver Relay." Each player was given a toothpick which he gripped firmly between his front teeth. The group was then divided into two lines. The first player of each team was given a Life Saver which he hung on the toothpick in his mouth. At the word "Go" he transferred the Life Saver to the toothpick of the second line without the use of hands. Of course, the team finishing first was declared the winner.

We had planned the approximate time required for each game so the entire evening would be filled. No time was allowed to drag between games. For refreshments we served the boys' standby—ice cream and cake. After refreshments the man of the house took all the guests home.

If your boy is at this difficult age don't hesitate to let him have a party. Plan a full evening of "boisterous" games like those mentioned above and I'm sure that both you and the boys will thoroughly enjoy the party. There was no damage to the house that a vacuum cleaner couldn't repair the next day.

For Lads and Lassies

A SPOOL PARTY

"Ooo Grandmother! Where did you ever get so many empty spools?" Bobby was kneeling in front of a drawer in Grandmother's sideboard.

"I've been saving them, Bobby, all winter long. I thought maybe you'd like to have a spool party this vacation."

"A spool party?" Bobby's eyes opened wide in wonder. "I've never even heard of one."

"All the better," said Grandmother, as she reached into the drawer for a handful of spools. "These short fat spools would be good to write the invitations on. I'm sure there are enough for that."

Bobby was eager as he dug through the full drawer of spools his grandmother had accumulated. After several tries, Bobby and his grandmother printed in small letters around the middle of the short fat spools,

Come to my spool party Friday at three P.M.
Bobby Halverson.

It was lots of fun passing out these spool invitations to the neighboring children with whom Bobby played during his summer vacation at Grandmother's.

During the days before the party Bobby cut many strips of cardboard one-half inch wide and three- and four-inches long. These were to be used during the party for building material. Then Bobby picked four small spools of equal size; painted one red, one green, one yellow, and the other blue. These were the family autos.

Friday afternoon the boys and girls arrived anxious to discover what a spool party would be like. As soon as all the guests arrived Bobby showed them a spool dog that Grandmother had shown him how to make. The head was cut out of cardboard tapering into a long neck which fitted into one end of the spool. The face was drawn with black crayon. At the other end of the spool emerged a long curved tail that looked as if it would wag any minute.

Four cardboard legs were glued to the sides of the spool. He made a surprisingly good-looking dog.

When Bobby told the children that they could make any kind of animal they wanted to, there was much excitement. In every corner of the room dogs, cats, lambs and cows were being created. When the animals were all finished, the youngsters built a spool pen by placing spools of equal size about three and one-half inches apart. The four-inch strips of cardboard were then put across the spools and held in place by small button-twist spools.

With the animals safely corralled, Grandmother explained the next game while Bobby built a series of bridges. For piers he used tall slender spools joined at the top with strips of cardboard. These strips can be scotch-taped to the tops of the spools to hold them in place. The piers were placed just far enough apart for one of the painted spool cars to roll through.

Then each child was given four tries to get the four spool autos, one at a time, through any space between the bridge piers. The red spool counted five points, the blue four, the green three, and the yellow two. If a car in going through knocked down part of the bridge the driver lost two points. It kept Grandmother busy keeping score through the fun and excitement of the game.

Grandmother then had a surprise ready. She brought out a bunch of larger spools, one for each child, and showed the children how to make spool wind-up cars.

In addition to the spools each child was given a button (underwear-button size), a rubber band, some match sticks and some cellulose tape. Then she instructed them to thread the rubber band through one hole in the button. It can be forced through with a pin if necessary. Then she put a match, with the head removed, through the loop so that the rubber band wouldn't slip out of the button. The other end of the rubber band was put through the spool and held there by a short piece of match stick. To keep this end from slipping Grandmother taped it to the end of the spool.

The car was all ready now to be wound up. The button served as a bearing. Soon each child discovered that if he twisted the crank or long match stick until the rubber band was tight and put the spool on the floor, the little car would run rapidly across the room. These were tops in fun, and much more exciting than the many commercial wind-up cars the children had bought.

While the youngsters were playing with their cars, Grandmother set the supper table. At each plate was a spool place-card and for a centerpiece Grandmother had transferred the spool animals, made earlier by the children, to the center of the table. To the boys and girls this was more attractive than the fanciest floral arrangement.

Supper consisted of baked potato, creamed chicken, and new peas. The dessert was the surprise. Grandmother had baked a big cake and decorated it to look like a huge spool.

At going-home time, the children gathered their animals and wind-up cars, declaring that this spool party was lots of fun. The youngsters were sure that from here on they would be on the watch for all empty spools.

BACK TO SCHOOL PARTY!

School days! What fun to see old friends and make new ones. Why not give a "Back to School" party so that your new friends and old friends can really get acquainted?

Like to play school? Almost everyone does. It's most fun when each one has a turn at playing "Teacher." Ask your newest friend to be "Teacher" for the first game.

The first class will be a Geography lesson. Give Teacher a stack of twenty-six cards, each of which bears one letter of the alphabet. Of course, you will have prepared these cards ahead of time. When Teacher holds up an "A" the first one to call out the name of a city beginning with "A" gets the "A" card. Next Teacher displays a "B" and the promptest one in naming a town beginning with "B" gets the "B" card. This continues until all twenty-six letters are distributed. The pupil who collects the largest number of letters becomes Teacher for the next game.

The next class may be a "Chemistry class" and Teacher will pass out a dozen small bottles filled with various liquids such as vinegar, peppermint, ammonia, tea, coffee, water, etc. Each bottle will bear only a number. Each pupil will try to identify the liquids by smell, writing the number of the bottle and his guess on a card. After each pupil has had sufficient time to "sniff" and write his answer, the pupil passes his list to his right hand partner. When the Teacher reads the correct list each pupil corrects the sheet before him. The boy or girl with the nearest correct list will be the next Teacher.

Spelling is a "must" for a good school. A spelling bee with motions adds a bit of zip. Instead of saying the vowels, when spelling a word, put in the following motions:

    a — raise the right hand
    e — raise the left hand
    i — point to your eye
    o — point to your mouth
    u — point to your neighbor
For instance to spell the word "tailor"
    T
    a — raise the right hand
    i — point to you eye
    l
    o — point to your mouth
    r

Anyone who spells a word incorrectly or says a vowel instead of making the right motion, drops out. The last one standing becomes Teacher for the Shorthand class.

All answers in this class are given with one or two letters of the alphabet. Answers may be written down and winner picked from cards.

    1. A foe ....NME (Enemy)
    2. Not full ....MT (Empty)
    3. A girl's name ....LC (Elsie)
    4. A composition ....SA (Essay)
    5. Not hard ....EZ (Easy)
    6. A state of joy ....XTC (Ecstasy)
    7. To surpass ....XL (Excel)

After this hilarious game, pupils and teachers alike will be ready for something to eat. Sandwiches, fruit, cake and paper cups of ice cream fit nicely into paper sacks to represent school bag lunches.

This Back to School party will cement friendships for the school days ahead and be a party to remember.

RAINBOW'S
POT OF GOLD

At the end of the rainbow, there's a pot of gold.
Everyone knows that. Let's have a rainbow
party and find the gold.

For invitations use gold-colored construction paper
with a rainbow in brilliant colors across the top, and
with the words —

> A hunting we will go
> For gold at Jim's house,
> Friday after school.

Now for the fun. Spread clues around the yard.
Number one reads:

> Perhaps you'll find it in the air,
> If not, look underneath the bear.

Some place on the grounds will be a small Teddy bear
seated calmly on this note:

> No you will not find it here,
> Search the shock and have no fear.

A shock of corn is an ideal hiding place. Even energetic
hunters will have to scramble to find a small note
reading:

> You will have to try once more;
> Look behind a barnyard door.

Here the note may read:

> If it's not in the stable
> Look beneath the kitchen table.

Under the kitchen table have a basket of little rubber
balls wrapped in gold foil; one for each hunter.

Use the balls to play the game of Bounce. Put an empty basket on a chair. Draw a line on the ground six feet away. Each one, in turn, stands on the line and bounces the ball on the ground and into the basket. Each player is given three trials. He wins a gold-wrapped penny each time the ball lands in the basket.

Now for a Ball Race. The players stand in a circle and are numbered 1, 2, 1, 2. The number ones make up one team and the twos make another team. Each player tries to throw the ball past the person standing next to him and into the hands of his own teammate.

At a signal the balls are started off in opposite directions. If there are few players, the balls should make three complete trips around to finish one race. The winner in two out of three races is Champion.

The balls change directions after each race. The game may be varied by throwing both balls in the same direction.

After all this activity try the Golden Shell game. Show a gold shell — a walnut shell wrapped in gold foil. Give each player a card and pencil. Tell him there are twenty objects hidden in that empty walnut shell. The winner, of course, is the one with the nearest correct list. It's amazing at the number of articles a walnut shell will hold. Here are suggestions.

Thumb tack, small tack, button, hair, bit of string, bit of cloth, rubber band, piece of sponge, short bobby pin, paper clip, small safety pin, scrap of paper, pencil eraser from end of pencil, finger nail clipping, small thimble (many tiny things can be crushed into the thimble), seed, grain of corn, oats, bit of egg shell, thread.

Try packing a walnut shell. You may be able to find even more things that will fit it.

For refreshments all will enjoy "Sloppy Joes" and Cokes topped off with a big dish of ice cream.

To finish off the party after refreshments ask the guests to wander around the yard — or any given area — and find as many golden objects as they can in ten minutes. The number will be surprising — a yellow leaf, a marigold, yellow grain, and don't forget to add some golden loot to the natural golden things, such as gold foil wrapped candy bars, or Hershey kisses, gold-wrapped peanuts or popcorn balls.

AN EXPLORER'S PARTY

Every male, whether he is six or sixty, is a potential Columbus. To explore makes any party a success.

A cave in your vicinity is a perfect setting for an exploration party. If there are no caves available perhaps there are rocky cliffs along a river bank or a nearby wooded area. Recently in our city a cave party was given in an underground tunnel adjoining the Art Institute.

A flat piece of limestone makes a perfect invitation. On the stone let your son print the words:

Come to the Explorer's party
To find adventure
After school on Friday
Jeans and old shoes are order of the day.

If the man of your house isn't available to go with the exploring party, be sure the lads are accompanied by some reliable older boy. Guests shouldn't wind up in the Lost and Found department of your local woods.

Before the explorers start on their journey, familiarize them with agates or quartz or some other stones that are found in your locality. In some sections of our country, the youngsters could hunt for Indian arrowheads. To give zest to the adventure promise that the one bringing back the largest collection (or the rarest arrowhead or the finest agate) will win a prize.

If a cave is your territory, offer a prize to the youngsters drawing the finest picture on the cave walls for posterity.

Give each youngster a tough manila bag to carry home his loot. Take your crew by car to the starting point of the exploration.

While they are gone gather together the wood for an outdoor fire and be ready when they return, with buns, wieners to roast, plenty of subterranean water (soft drinks) to quench their thirst, and prehistoric snow (ice cream). Be sure you have plenty of food, because exploring whets the appetite of even the most dainty eater.

After the meal around the fire, have a display of found treasures. Let the lads themselves study the stones or arrowheads or whatever, and discuss and decide on the various merits. Perhaps several prizes might be given — one for the largest collection, the prettiest, as well as the finest. A scout knife would make an excellent prize. For the boys who don't win something special, a prize could be given for extra effort.

By this time, we'll guarantee your explorers will be ready to go home. Before you go, be sure the camp fire is completely out. Let the boys participate in putting it out — they will learn a lesson in woodsmanship.

JACK AND JILL'S
CLOWN PARTY

Parties for boys or for girls in the grades are not too hard to plan but woe to the mother of boy and girl twins. Her job to plan a birthday party for her Jack and Jill that will please them both takes a bit of doing.

Mrs. Grady faced this problem. She wanted a gay, happy party where the boys wouldn't spend their time teasing the girls, and the girls wouldn't tauntingly sing, "Jackie's got a girl friend, Jackie's got a girl friend."

Her solution was a clown party. All youngsters love a clown, and the twins were enthusiastic while they cut invitations in the shape of a clown's hat on which they printed:

> A-clowning we will go
> At Jack and Jill's
> Friday after school.

When the boys and girls arrived bubbling with joy of anticipation, they were shown a large gay-looking carton which the twins had decorated with clown's faces and bright-colored balls. Their curiosity was intense and they were delighted to discover in this box a supply of wide ruffs of gay-colored crepe paper and tall white crepe paper hats with bright tassels—one for each guest.

Dressed in this attire each youngster caught the gay spirit of clowndom, and the party was on its way. The young clowns were seated around card tables on which was a supply of paper coffee cups with handles, some cone-shaped paper cups, and paper baking cups. Also paste, crayons and scissors. They were also shown a completed puppet clown for a pattern and each one was asked to make one. The pattern had a face drawn on the coffee cup with an extra handle added for the other ear. The cone-shaped paper cup decorated with many colored dots made the hat. The pleated paper baking cup made the ruff.

The children were enthusiastic over their creations. They discovered that by sticking a hand in the paper cup the clowns could be made to turn their heads, bow and do other clownish maneuvers.

The boy and girl whose clowns were voted the funniest became captains for the next game.

After this bit of quiet activity the youngsters were ready for some exercise. Jack and Jill took their friends outdoors for a hoop-jumping contest. For this contest the twins had prepared beforehand a number of large hoops made of stout wire and covered with red tissue paper.

The captains chose their teams so that an even number were on each side. There was a hoop for each guest. The captains held the hoop tilted so that a child running from a given goal could easily jump through the hoop bursting the paper covering as he did so. The side going through the line first was declared the winner. This was a very exciting game, not too difficult but loads of fun.

At the end of this game the hoops were used for a hoop-rolling contest. The boys competed against the girls. Each member of the winning team was given two bags of popcorn, one of which he gave to a member of the losing team.

Now came a chance to show off a bit. The young clowns all sat in a circle and each one took a turn at clowning.

Each clown performed his funniest stunt while the young-sters applauded vigorously.

The boy and girl clown who won first place as "fun-niest" became the "twirler" in the old game of "Statue." The boy twirler grabbed the right hand of each boy and swung him around three times. The clowns held the po-sitions in which they landed. The twirler looked them over and picked the most interesting one to be the next twirler. The girl clown twirled all the girls and judged her group.

To have a quiet game before lunch the clowns seated themselves in a circle for a game of "Circus." The first clown started the game by saying, "I went to the circus to see an anteater." The next in line repeats, "I went to the circus to see an anteater," and adds an animal begin-ning with the letter "b" as "bear." The third in line might say, "I went to the circus and saw an anteater, a bear, and a clown." One who fails to think of an object beginning with the next letter of the alphabet goes to the center of the circle.

By the time only a few were left competing, lunch was ready. Jack and Jill led their guests to the dining room for refreshments. For place cards balloons were used. A balloon bearing the name of a guest was tied to the back of each chair. Shouts of laughter greeted this new idea while the guests scrambled for their seats.

The traditional ice cream became jolly clowns—a scoop of ice cream on a pineapple slice with bits of maraschino cherries for roguish eyes and mouth, and a whole cherry for a bulbous nose. Cone-shaped paper drinking cups with a red tassel on top perched on top of the clown face, added the last touch to the clownish appearance. Little frosted squares of white cake were dotted with tiny red candies.

The party guests were tired but happy. They gathered up their puppets to take home as favors. They were sure nothing could be more fun than such a jolly clown party.

INVITE THE PARENTS TOO!

The next time your small fry wants a party for his gang, don't be scared of a rough house. Just answer, "Certainly." Then make it an early evening party, invite his friends *and their parents*. Include all small brothers and sisters. You'll have quite a crowd, we'll admit, but we can guarantee that if you plan your games right, you'll have a party that will be long remembered not only by your young son but his friends and their parents as well.

The secret of the success of such a party is, of course, to have games that all ages can enter into, and you'd be surprised how many such games there are.

A good opener for such a party is the "Nose Game." Hang an old sheet in an open doorway. Tacks stuck into the top of the doorjamb don't show and will hold a substantial cord. Then fasten big safety pins into the top edge of the sheet and pin them over the cord. This makes a very satisfactory draw curtain. In the sheet make two slits, one big enough for an adult to stick his nose through, the other a suitable height for the shorter guests. (This curtain can be prepared ahead of time and drawn across the doorway for this one game.)

Gather all the women on the back side of the curtain. Then ask the men if they are sure they can recognize their own wives. They'll be very confident of their ability.

Warn the children not to help their Dads. Then have each woman take a turn at sticking her nose through the slit in the sheet. It is surprisingly difficult for a man, no matter how long he has been married, to recognize his wife by her nose. After the choosing is completed let the women join the men who have claimed them. Most of the men will have some other fellow's wife.

Then hustle the kids behind the sheet. Make the men pick their own kids—don't let the women help. Mothers have washed those faces so often they are better choosers than the men. One father of four children at a recent party of ours wound up with claiming only one of his four off-spring—the other three proved to belong to some of the other guests. But then no one had his own family intact.

A stunt that looks very easy but is really hard to do is called the "Broomstick Game." Lay a broomstick on the floor. Place your elbow next to the broom handle and measure the distance to your finger tips. Put an apple on that spot. Then kneel on the broomstick, keeping both hands on the stick, and pick up the apple with your teeth. Chances are you'll land on your nose first try. The kids love to see Mother and Dad try this one.

To find the richest person in the crowd, divide the group into two teams. Give each one a bowl of uncooked navy beans and a spoon. Each one stands in front of a mirror and takes a spoonful of beans and by looking into the mirror, tries to drop them into an empty milk bottle which he holds on top of his head. More beans will go on the floor and down the neck than into the bottle. Then each one counts the beans he has been successful in getting into the bottle. Each bean is worth $100,000. Keep the resulting figures from your income tax man—he'd be staggered at the worth of your guests.

Let the parents watch the kids in a bottle wrestle. It can be played in any living room and nothing will be damaged. Divide the kids into pairs, matching them according to size and weight. The partners face each other on opposite sides of a milk bottle which stands on the floor. They place their hands on each other's shoulders. Then each one tries by pushing and pulling to make his partner knock over the milk bottle. The one knocking over the bottle or losing his balance loses the match. This is a very strenuous game that takes a small space in which to play.

"In-betweeners" always like to play a trick on someone. "Fancy Stepping" answers this urge. A group of guests who do not know the stunt are assembled in one room. Then the host places four objects a little distance apart across the living-room floor. Good things to use are a whole raw egg, a plant, a cut glass vase, and a silver tea pot—the more fragile the things the better. Then a "victim" is brought into the room and told that he will be blindfolded and will have to step over the fragile objects without touching them. To help him gauge the distance, permit him to step over the articles with his eyes open. Much atmosphere is created by repeated cautionings as to the value and fragility of the objects. The victim is then blindfolded, spun around three times and started on his perilous course. While he is being spun the objects are quietly removed from the floor. The victim then starts out working diligently to step over the things that are no longer there. It is terrifically funny to watch people stepping high, wide, and handsome over a bare spot on the floor.

A game that rates tops in hilarity is a "Costume Race." Choose two Dads to head the two teams. Have each team include some mothers as well as half the kids. Then present each captain with a suitcase of clothes. A skirt or loose beach slacks, a flower hat and a pair of mittens make a hilarious costume. The object of the game is to have each contestant dress in the clothes, then race out the front door around the house and in the back door carrying the suitcase. When he reaches the starting point he takes off the clothes and repacks them and passes the bag to the next man on the team. The excitement and hilarity in the dressing and packing reduces the onlookers to limpness from laughter.

Of course, the team completing the race first is the winner. At one of our recent parties one father, with tears of laughter running down his cheeks, remarked, "I thought this was a kids' party. I haven't had so much fun in years."

We seldom give prizes at any of our family parties. We have learned through experience that in games where everyone participates the fun of winning seems to satisfy without a prize. To avoid any unnecessary delays we always make a list of games ahead of time and collect the props needed for each game. As our games do not call for expensive equipment, we only need to assemble from around the house the props needed. As each game is finished we refer to our list, kept in a handy spot, for the next game. The youngsters soon spot the list and at the end of each game race to it to see "What's next?" As our list contains only the names of the games, it serves as a teaser.

Keep your refreshments simple and serve them buffet style. The children like to sit on the floor to eat and the parents enjoy eating from trays or plates held in their laps. The informality of it all will please everyone.

The advantages of the family parties are quite apparent. The kids have a rollicking good time. You, as hostess, get the cooperation of the parents in promoting the games and keeping the youngsters' exuberant spirits in check. And the kids themselves, besides the good times, learn how to be host and guest and learn the fellowship that comes from hospitality. With our family of growing boys we have had many such parties and every one of them has proved to be a howling success, and we do mean "Howling."

ADD SOME SPICE

Family gatherings! How Grandmother loves them. And Mother and Dad too. But how about the teen-agers? Do they look forward to these occasions with enthusiasm? Maybe your young people aren't slow about expressing their dislike of "sitting around the house all day, listening to Aunt Minnie crab." But if they haven't said so, we can be almost certain that they avoid such occasions whenever they possibly can.

Of course, when the children are little, they receive a great deal of attention from the adults in the family. After the cute age, they are often overlooked in family gatherings. The women exchange recipes and discuss the church circles; the men talk of the world situation, or business trends. It's dull for teen-agers you must admit.

The next time your clan gathers for one of these family get-togethers, try some games. One game that will include every one, young and old, is called "Who Am I?" To start the game one person thinks of a character either fictional or real — alive or dead — American or foreign. The rest of the family take turns asking questions which can be answered by "yes" or "no." One person asks questions until he gets a "No" answer. Then the next person takes a turn. At our last family gathering this game made a hit, and we were all amazed at the teen-ager's fund of general information.

"Memory Selections" is another game that is lots of fun. This is where Grandmother and Grandfather shine.

One member of the family is the challenger. He may give a quotation from some specified field such as the Bible, poetry, or some famous speech. Or if he wishes, he can announce before beginning that he will use quotations from any source. When the challenger has recited his chosen quotation the family, one at a time, takes turns in guessing the source from which the quotation was taken. The one who guesses the correct source then takes his turn as challenger and gives a quotation to be identified.

In an easier form of this game, the challenger may quote a line of poetry. Other members of the gathering in turn try to add the next line. For instance, the challenger says "Early to bed and early to rise." A guesser can reply "Makes a man healthy, wealthy, and wise."

If your family is musical, try Musical Memories. The challenger hums a line or two of a song. The guesser will then respond with the rest of the song or its title. Limit the field to old songs, popular songs, or even well-known hymns, and the whole family will be interested.

"Wrong Capitals" is always fun. The challenger names a state capital placing it in the wrong state. The one to his right gets first chance to correct the challenger. For instance, the challenger may say "St. Paul is the capital of Iowa." The next in turn will say "Wrong. St. Paul is the capital of Minnesota." Then he announces that "Austin is the capital of New Mexico." The one to his right must then try to locate Austin correctly and so on. One of the players may occasionally trip the others by placing a capital in the right state, which adds a lot to the hilarity of the game.

Are you a member of a mechanically minded family? If so, try Car Scramble. The challenger names some make of car or tractor. Next in line names a car beginning with the last letter of the first car named. For instance, if the challenger say "Buick," the next person may say "Kaiser." This is an interesting game because someone is sure to remember old makes of cars forgotten by almost everyone.

At your next family gathering try these games or some similar one, and we'll guarantee that your young people will be willing guests.

A BLOCK PARTY

Did you ever hear of block parties? Let us recommend them. They are something different in the way of parties. We live in a new district and, like many new districts, there are many children. In our block the children are all about the same age, and as a result the parents and children have become well acquainted.

Children have birthdays, and birthdays mean parties—first one home and then another. The novelty had worn off. Wasn't there something new and entirely different to do? We all got together to plan and the block-party idea was born.

Our house became Union Station for the evening. At six o'clock the travelers (children) arrived ready for the first part of their journey. Under the care of the Conductor and Engineer (entertainment committee) all embarked for Hawaii (a neighbor's house across the street). In true Hawaiian style each guest was presented with a paper flower lei to wear for travel. While the guests nibbled slices of fresh pineapple and crackers the young hostess, who belongs to a dancing class, entertained with a Hawaiian dance.

Next came the long trip to China. Here Chinese lanterns were everywhere. By lantern light the travelers ate big plates of Chow-Mein on the spacious back porch. Then they hit the road again for Turkey, that land of romance and mystery. Entering the home of the Sultan, the travelers were cordially welcomed by the sons and daughters of the household, who were attractively dressed in Turkish costumes. A serving of date pudding completed the ample meal the travelers had gathered along the way.

Then followed an uneventful passage to America and incidentally a visit to an Indian village (another home). Here "Heap Big Chief" and his tribe gave their Indian dances, showed their wonderful rugs, beads and weapons, and for a finish served some of their native food, Popped Corn.

On the wing again—a flying trip to Union Station, point of departure—to play some games children in other countries enjoy.

First came a Chinese game called "Dragon's Tail." All the children lined up, hands on shoulders of the child ahead. The first child became the head of the dragon and the last the tail. The hostess called out, "One-two-three-go!" At the signal the head tried to catch the tail. In and out around the amusement room wove the dragon (line of youngsters), the head trying valiantly to tag the tail. The whole body moved with the head and remained unbroken. If the head caught the tail that child continued to be head. If the body broke first, he became the tail. The very minute someone let go, the Dragon died. This Chinese game was strenuous and hilarious.

After this exciting game it was good to sit quietly in a circle. Indian corn was used for this popular Indian game. One child hid the kernels of corn in one of his hands, and standing before another child in the circle said, "Guess how many?" He asked his question first of one child and then of another in the group until he had been all around the circle. Of course, the child who guessed the correct number, or the nearest correct, won, and became "IT" for the next game.

Next was a "Fish Game" commonly played in Denmark. Folding chairs were placed in pairs around the room. And the children grouped themselves into pairs. One couple became "IT" and were named "Whales." The other couples seated themselves in these chairs. Each couple, other than the "Whales," secretly selected the name of a fish. The whales wandered about the room calling out from time to time the name of some fish. Each fish called left his chair and marched after the whales. If the whales called out, "The Ocean is calm," everyone left his chair and followed the whales. When the whales called out, "The Ocean is stormy," all the couples raced to get chairs. The left-over couple became whales. This Danish fish game proved to be popular with our young Americans.

Next we enjoyed a Mexican game called "Bread and Cheese." The Buyer stood in the center of the ring of children and asked Tommy, "Where do they sell bread and cheese?" Tommy pointing to Sally standing at the far side of the ring, said, "There it is very cheap." The Buyer then repeated his question of Sally. Meanwhile Tommy changed places with Mary who was directly opposite him in the circle. The Buyer then tried to dash into one of the empty spaces before either Tommy or Mary could get there. If he reached the spot first, then the one left out became Buyer.

From Mexico we jumped to Alaska for an "Alaskan Guessing Game." John became "IT" and was given twenty small sticks of wood. The other children closed their eyes tightly while John arranged the sticks in a series of groups on the ground. When John called "ready," the other players shouted out their guess as to the number of sticks on the ground. The one who first guessed the correct number of sticks became the next "IT."

Not to overlook our own country the children were next introduced to the good old American game of "Wall

Ball." The players numbered off, and scattered about. Number one player tossed the ball against the cement wall and, after the ball left his hand, called a number. The player whose number was called had to catch the ball on the first bounce. If he was successful, he threw it and called a number—if he didn't catch the ball on the first bounce, the original thrower threw it again.

By this time the curfew was ringing and our neighborhood children returned home voting the "Block Party" the most fun of all.

THE FIRST BOY-GIRL PARTY

The first mixed party! This is a red letter day on any calendar and it must be something special to remember. Dropping clothespins in a bottle and pinning a tail on a donkey is small-fry stuff—and just doesn't make a party for teen-agers.

So why not invite these shy young swains and their giggling girl friends over for a Fun Frolic and plan the games so that for this night Fun is King.

Here is a good mixer to start the fun and get the young guests in a party mood.

When the girls have removed their wraps in one room, the boys in another, give each one a paper sack, No. 20, in which you have cut notches for eyes, nose and mouth, and crayoned a large number just below the chin. A few pencil marks in the right places make these masks smiling, grotesque, or what have you. Slip these sacks on over the head. When the fellows and gals return to the living room, provide each with a card and pencil, offering a reward to the one who first identifies each paper head. Sounds easy—but you'd be surprised how long it takes to make such a list and how thoroughly it melts icy shyness. As a reward let the first gal and the first boy to complete the nearest correct list be the first couple to try "Double Handcuffs."

Be ready with two strings forty inches long. Tie each end of one of the strings around the boy's wrists. The second string is passed between the boy's string and his body and the ends of it tied to each of the girl's wrists, thus linking the two together. The object is for the couple to free themselves without breaking or untying the strings. It's loads of fun to watch the couple struggle to get free, stepping through the loop, putting it over their heads, and the like.

Satisfy the crowd's urge to try it by handcuffing each lad and lass together. Sooner or later some bright youngster will discover the trick, and the gang will be much disconcerted with its simplicity. The handcuffed boy picks up his string, puts it under the string on the inside of the girl's wrist, over her hand, down the back of her hand and under the string. Presto, the couple is free, although the strings are unbroken and still fastened to the wrists.

When the excitement from this game has died down, announce "How Green you are." One person leaves the room. While he is gone the gang decides what he is to do when he is called back. It might be decided that he is to smell a flower on the table, or take off his shoes, or turn out a light. As soon as he responds to the call "ready," the crowd sings "How Green you are" to the tune of "Auld Lang Syne" while he is trying to discover what is expected of him. When he gets nearer the object involved the crowd sings louder, when he gets farther away the singing grows softer. This stunt is loads of fun. It is amazing how complicated the stunts can be and still be accomplished.

A game that is ridiculous to watch as well as do is called "Cotton Bowl." Place a large empty glass bowl in the center of a small table—a card table will do. Scatter around the bowl a quantity of cotton balls—they can be purchased at a drug store. Blindfold each contestant, whirl him around three times and then hand him a large wooden spoon, announcing that he will have one minute to see how many cotton balls he can spoon into the bowl. Since the balls have no weight, many times the contestant will spoon furiously with nothing in his spoon. Let a score-keeper count the total number of balls the girls get into the bowl and the number the boys get into it. The side with the greatest number wins the game.

Almost everyone is familiar with tit tat toe, the game in which two players, using a drawn block of nine squares, compete to finish a line of Os or Xs before the opponent blocks the line. Here is a game of human tit tat toe that is fun for teen-agers. Place three chairs in a row—three chairs directly behind each of the first three chairs to make a second row. Complete the square by putting three more chairs directly behind the first two rows. You now have a tit-tat-toe square made of nine chairs. The first girl player sits in any chair of her choice. A boy player takes a chair of his choice, keeping in mind that he must sit so as to keep the girls from completing a row of three girls. The next girl tries to sit so as to continue the girls' line and block the boys. Boys and girls alternate taking seats until either the girls or boys complete an unbroken line of three or, as is sometimes the case, all lines are blocked. Then the cat gets that game. The boys and girls will want to play this game over several times especially if the score is in favor of first one and then the other.

By this time the crowd will be ready for a lively circle game called "Face to Face." The partners stand facing each other in one large circle. One odd player stands in the center and calls, "Face to face," "Back to back," "Face to face," "Back to back," the players taking their positions accordingly. When he calls, "All change," the players must take new partners. The center player tries to get one too. If he succeeds, the person left without a partner must go into the center and give the commands.

About now announce that lunch is ready and the couples facing each other in the preceding game automatically become partners for lunch, which will be ready to eat buffet style. A substantial menu for these insatiable appetites can be sandwiches made with tuna-fish salad in Parker House rolls, crisp potato chips, dill pickles, with heaping dishes of ice cream, and generous slices of devil's-food cake. Be sure your supply of food is adequate because the guys at this party, if not the gals, will be back for seconds and maybe thirds.

Before they leave, these young sprouts will be asking when they can come again for another such get-together.

ENTERTAINING THE
SUB-SUB-DEBS

"Mother, can I have a party?"

"Certainly," I answered our young son.

Then I hesitated. Parties—we'd always had plenty of them. But now with the young son in High School, this wouldn't be any little boy affair.

"What kind of a party would you like?" I asked very casually.

"Oh there're about six fellows I'd like to invite," he said, and added slowly, "and about six girls."

This couldn't be a dance because many of this crowd were not yet accomplished dancers, neither did they care much about bridge. But we can try anything once so I told him to invite the youngsters and we'd plan games for their entertainment. Now I look back and wonder why all the dither. Just in case some of you are up against the same proposition let me tell you how it worked out.

John invited the girls by telephone and when each girl accepted he told her one of the boys would call for her. Then he invited the boys and asked each one to see that a certain girl arrived safely. This plan settled the couple problem to the satisfaction of all concerned.

The first game of the evening was "Amnesia." Beforehand we had written on slips of paper the names of famous people; movie stars, radio comedians, comic-strip characters, and the like. One of these slips was pinned on the

126

back of each guest. The name on the slip was unknown to the one wearing it. According to the game, each guest had lost his memory and was to learn his identity himself. He was forbidden to remove the paper from his back or to look into a mirror. He could ask questions of the other guests, but only questions that could be answered by "yes" or "no." With everyone asking questions of everyone else the ice was soon broken. From then on the evening was a gay affair.

The next game proved to be so much fun, they asked to play it a second time. The players were all seated in a circle. John started a three-beat rhythm and everyone joined in. On the count of one, hands were all clapped on knees; on the count of two, hands were clapped together in front; and on the three, all snapped their fingers with arms outstretched parallel to their shoulders. At the count of three John named a common noun such as "elephant." Without breaking the one, two, three rhythm the girl next gave a noun beginning with "t" such as "teacher." The new word had to begin with "t" because that was the last letter of the previous word mentioned. The noun must be given on the third beat of the rhythm. The one who couldn't think of a noun quick enough dropped out of the game until the winner was finally determined.

"Progressive Fortunes" is a lot of fun especially with a crowd of boys and girls. The guests were all seated in a circle. Each one was given a long piece of paper and a pencil. The strips of paper were cut beforehand of uniform size. Each guest wrote his name at the top of the paper and folded it over far enough to conceal the name.

He then passed it to his right-hand neighbor who in turn wrote out a four-word description of his past life. This caused a lot of merriment and, of course, the youngsters loved to make it wicked. This, in turn, was again folded over so that the writing was covered and it was again passed to the right.

Then John asked the crowd to write a four-word description of the one he or she liked best. Some of these turned out to be quite "flowery" while others were sarcastic depending upon the nature of the writer.

After folding over these were passed to the right and each participant stated in four words what he thought of himself. There was much hilarity among the youngsters as they described themselves.

Once again the papers were folded and passed to the right. Plans for his future were now written in four words by each guest, and the papers were passed to the right-hand neighbor who kept it. Then each youngster took turns reading aloud the paper he held which was supposed to be the fortune of the one whose name appeared at the top of each sheet. Of course, these fortunes, being the product of many minds, were extremely funny.

Before we realized it was time for refreshments. Believing that no boy or girl has ever quite had his fill of ice-cream sundaes, we decided to let each guest make his own—as many as he could hold. On the dining-room table were all the "makings" for the sundaes. There were two large bowls of bulk ice cream—vanilla and chocolate; a quantity of quartered bananas for banana splits, pitchers of chocolate and butterscotch syrup; dishes of preserved cherry and strawberry sauces; two dishes of nuts, pecans and cashews; a bowl of whipped cream and a dish of maraschino cherries for trimming. There were also assorted homemade cookies. Card tables were provided at which the guests sat while enjoying their sundaes.

The youngsters had a grand time concocting their own sundaes, some of which, needless to say, were very original. When the evening was over many of the guests had four sundaes to their credit.

Don't hesitate to let your "fourteeners" have a party. It's lots of fun for the parents as well as the youngsters.

AN OUTDOOR
MYSTERY PARTY

August — the perfect time to solve a mystery. Invite your friends to help.

LOST, STRAYED OR STOLEN
a valuable object that's
Red, White, and Black,
and Green all over.
The search will be at our
house on Saturday afternoon.

When the guests arrive give each boy a Sherlock Holmes' cardboard badge cut in the shape of Holmes' pipe. To each girl goes a Watson badge cut in the shape of Watson's cap.

Explain that a Valuable Object has been stolen and that it's up to the sleuths to discover if it was stolen by male or female. Why it was taken. Who was the thief? What the Valuable Object is, and where it is hidden.

To solve the question as to whether the thief is male or female, all the detectives line up ready for a race to the far side of the yard. It being conceded that boys run faster than girls, handicap the lads by asking them to run backwards. If the girls win the race it is a sure indication that it was a girl who stole the Valuable Object. If the boys win, then, of course, a boy did the stealing.

Why was it taken? To determine this important point do a tail-catching stunt. For real sport let half the boys and half the girls line up in a single file, each one holding on to the waist of the person in front of him.

The other half of the sleuths form the second line. The object of this game is for the head of each line to catch the tail of the other line. The sleuth who first catches the tail of the other line, can give his idea of why the Valuable Object was taken.

The first race decided the sex of the thief. The second stunt revealed the reason for the theft, and now comes the identity of the thief. Give each player a sheet of stiff paper and a pencil. Ask each one to draw his favorite cartoon character. (Female if your race indicated it was a female, or male if that was so indicated.) You may discover the makings of a fine artist for policework. It creates much hilarity when it is announced that the best drawn cartoon is the thief.

Now as to a guess as to what the Valuable Object is. The guesses will come fast and furious. Remind the players of the clue on the invitation "Red, white, black, and green all over." The first one to guess that the missing Valuable Object is a watermelon can lead the detectives on the Big Search.

Hand the leader an envelope containing the first clue for the hunt, which says "Great oaks from little acorns grow." This will head the crowd for an oak tree. If your yard contains no oaks, better make it "Down by the apple tree" or some tree you do have. The next clue is found on a low branch of the tree in a big white envelope. Its message "The Valuable Object takes lots of water" will send your group to the pump or well. Here lies another clue which is only a number such as 435-567.

Some bright detective will soon realize the number given is the license number of your dad's car. On the top of the car will be found another envelope saying "The corn and It are often together." That will suggest that perhaps it is near the corn crib.

But here only will be found another envelope which may say,

> Mr. Finney had a turnip
> And it grew behind the barn,

And it grew, and it grew,
And the turnip did no harm.

Somewhere behind the barn the last envelope will
be found with these or similar words of wisdom, "Face
west, walk twenty steps forward. Make ¼ turn right
and take two steps backward. Make a right turn and
take 60 long steps forward. Turn right and dig." Buried
deep in the pile of hay will be the Valuable Object —
a big ripe watermelon.

Lug it back to the house for Mother to cut and serve
all the daring detectives who found the Valuable Object.
Perhaps she'll have sandwiches, potato chips and pop
to go with it.

After all the detectives are "full up" finish the afternoon off with a Watermelon Rolling contest. Divide
the detectives into four teams of equal numbers. Place
four watermelons on a starting line. At a signal each
leader will push the watermelon with his head to a
given goal across the lawn, turn around and push it
back to the starting line. Then the second player will
take his turn. The team finishing first wins the relay
and will be declared the champion Detectives of the
afternoon.

INVITE THE GANG IN

Have you an extremist in your home—a budding teen-ager extremely shy one minute and extremely bold the next—who wants to have a group of his fellow extremists in for a party?

If so don't stop him. Give him all the help you can, for he is bound to benefit by frequent social contacts. These contacts will eventually whittle down his extremes to a comfortable-to-live-with pattern that'll be much easier on the family.

As a rule the thirteen- or fourteen-year-old is too young to like bridge or ball-room dancing, while a program of children's games are much beneath his interests. However, games that recognize the youngster's interest in the opposite sex usually appeal to the shy boy and the boy-conscious girl.

A party with a theme always arouses anticipation and interest. "Shipwrecked" is such a party and we found it a lot of fun. The guests were invited to come dressed in clothes they had grabbed at three A.M. when the U.S.S. "Romance" was sinking. When the castaways arrived at our desert island they were garbed in everything from bath-robes to raincoats.

In keeping with the party theme we decorated the walls to represent a desert island. Huge pieces of wrapping paper painted with palm trees, tropical plants and birds and a wild tangle of weird tropical flowers covered the walls. Twisted green crepe paper hanging from the ceiling changed our living room into a semi-darkened jungle.

The unusual costumes and unusual jungle atmosphere immediately absorbed the attention of the youngsters and prevented that "stiff before the party starts" moment dreaded by most young people. As soon as the guests had gathered, the young host handed each guest a blank card. On it the guests had to write the color of the eyes of each one present. The girls were thrilled to have the boys take such particular notice of their eyes. This proved to be an excellent mixer.

To pick partners for the next game we tried this stunt. The boys gathered in one room and the girls in an adjoining room. A sheet curtained the doorway between the two rooms. The boys' room was darkened. In the other room we turned on bright lights directly back of the sheet. Then each girl walked between the light and the sheet. The boys chose their partners from the shadow on the sheet.

Because the shipwrecked people had lost their wardrobes, each boy was given several newspapers and a supply of pins. Then each boy made a dress for the partner he had chosen. He chose his own style of dress, tore the papers at will, and pinned a dress of paper on his lady.

Of course the girls were ready with plenty of suggestions. You'd be amazed at some of the newspaper creations turned out by these male dressmakers. A prize was awarded for the most attractive, the most unusual and the most skillful.

Very appropriate on a desert island was the hunt for the lost lover. Guests were seated in a circle with "IT" blindfolded in the center. "IT" groped about in search of a seated guest, then dropped to his knees and said to the one seated, "Are you my lost lover?" The victim answered with a disguised voice. He was asked to bark like a dog, meow like a cat, groan, etc., as "IT" tried to recognize who he was. One guess was allowed. If it was correct the victim took "IT"'s place. If not, "IT" tried again.

Youngsters of this age are always very news conscious, so it was fun to tell them that the morning papers wished to carry a full account of their party. We requested each one to answer in full the questions asked on the slip of paper handed him. However, each question was to be answered with two words beginning with the writer's first and last initials. We allowed five minutes for answering questions. The slips were then passed to the neighbor on the right who read them aloud. Good questions for this game are:

1. Where born?
2. What did father say?
3. Your first words?
4. Favorite sport?
5. Favorite food?
6. Pet peeve?
7. Secret ambition?
8. Type of sweetheart you like?
9. Your opinion of this party?
10. Your opinion of your host or hostess?

After this we asked the youngsters if they would like to do a bit of spooning. Lacking any volunteers we picked three couples. The partners were seated on opposite sides of the table and each was given a spoon. The spoons were tied together with about eight inches of string. Then each contestant was given a dish of ice cream. The object of the game was to see which couple could finish their ice cream without breaking the string. At a signal the race began. A broken string disqualified a couple. Winners were awarded wooden spoons purchased at the dime store.

All young people love to have their fortunes told. They liked the "Yarn of the Future." We had prepared for this beforehand by tying a written fortune every two feet on a ball of yarn. Then we rewound the ball adding extra yarn so that the paper fortunes wouldn't show. The host tossed the ball to a guest who unwound until he came to the first paper. He took it off then threw the ball to someone else. This continued until each guest had a paper. Then they took turns reading aloud. Here are some fortune suggestions that the teen-agers enjoyed:

1. Never get married on the thirty-second day of the month.
2. Don't get killed in the dark of the moon—it's fatal.
3. You'll soon be dead—dead wrong.
4. Don't watch the clock so closely—it may strike.
5. It's unlucky for you to drown on Friday the thirteenth.
6. You'll shine in society—if you don't powder your nose.
7. Don't cultivate a taking way—your friends may miss things.
8. Beware of courtships—they often sink.
9. Your rich relatives will soon leave you—but they won't leave you much.
10. If you're looking for love see "l" in the dictionary.

If you want to have some fun at refreshment time arrange an ice-cream bar. It's easy to do. On the dining-room table we put several bowls filled with balls of ice cream —one vanilla, one chocolate, and the other peppermint. We had one pitcher of chocolate sauce, another of butterscotch and a third of marshmallow cream. A dish of nuts and one of maraschino cherries completed the supplies. At the other end of the table we put a supply of sherbet glasses, spoons and napkins.

Each one became his own soda jerker. There's something in each of us that craves to mix fancy sundaes. You'll be surprised at the concoctions teen-agers will mix and also at the number they are able to consume. It solves the refreshment problem delightfully for all concerned.

A BEACH PARTY!

When the lads and lassies of Lake Harriet's Junior Yacht Club decided to have a get-together they didn't reckon on the ingenuity of the girls in the crowd. After much speculation and planning the girls concluded that in spite of the frozen lake, the howling of the Minnesota winds and the drifting snow they would stage a beach party as nearly as possible like the beach parties of the summer vacation days.

The invitations aroused plenty of curiosity and anticipation. The girls cut circles of construction paper and colored them to represent beach balls. On these were the printed invitations:

Beach party at 2121 Harriet Avenue
January 10th at 6:30 P.M.
Come loll on the beach, forget
the ice and snow and relive our summer fun.

"What are those crazy girls up to?" the boys wondered, while the girls, buzzing with secrecy, transferred the atmosphere of last summer's beach into Jane's comfortable amusement room. By using tempera paint (because tempera paint washes off), one wall of the room became a stretch of sandy beach with an occasional fir tree in the background.

On the opposite wall a couple of C and X sailboats floated gracefully on the blue waters. Upon the arrival of the guests the hostesses were in for a surprise. When the guests removed their overcoats and galoshes it was discovered they were wearing bright-colored play clothes and gay summer togs.

The picnic meal was set out buffet style on an outdoor table sheltered by a bright-colored marquee. The meal itself smacked of good old summertime—fried chicken, crisp potato chips, fresh fruit salad, followed with a dessert of ice-cream cones.

With such a setting it was only natural that during the meal the conversation drifted to the funny events of last summer—how Scott rammed a hole in Bob's boat and was dubbed the poorest helmsman—how Sally rammed the dock instead of leaving it astern and heading up to make a landing—how many times Dale tipped over and who won the regatta trophy.

After the meal the girls brought out the summer sports. First was a game of "Beach Ball." The guests formed a circle and were numbered 1, 2, 1, 2, and so on around the circle. The players numbered 1 became one team and had a blue beach ball; those numbered 2 were the opposing team and were given a red ball. Jane explained that the balls were to be passed to team members only. This meant that each player threw the ball past the person standing next to him and into the hands of his own team mate immediately beyond.

At a signal the balls were started off in opposite directions. The balls had to make three complete trips around the circle to finish one race. The balls changed directions after each race; that is, the team of players after passing its ball three times around to the right for the first race, passed it three times around to the left for the second race, and around to the right again for the last. The team winning two out of three races was declared champion.

Large colored balloons can be substituted for beach

balls. This game is lots of fun whether played on a beach or at a beach party in your amusement room.

A game of "Horseshoe" is always good on the beach. In place of driving stakes into the sand the girls used a child's game of horseshoe, with the stakes on metal standards and hard rubber horseshoes. These rubber shoes are really much harder to throw than the kind Old Dobbin wore. Nevertheless, the same rules applied—game was fifty points. Ringing the stake counted three points. If the player made a ringer with both shoes he was credited with six points. Points were awarded also for position. The nearest one to the stake scored one point. If both nearest belonged to the same player he got two points. A combination of one ringer and one shoe nearest the stake counted four points. Only one player scored in a turn. If both players made ringers each canceled the other. If the horseshoes of opponents were equidistant from the stake no points were awarded for either of the players. First play in the next turn was given to the member of the winning team at the opposite stake.

For the golf enthusiasts the next game on the program was "Clock Golf." Jane drew on the floor, with chalk, a circle fifteen feet in diameter, and numbered it around its circumference like a clock face. She then placed a tin can, about four inches in diameter, in the center of the circle. So that the balls would roll into the can she fitted a wide sloping cardboard collar around the can. Then she gave each guest a golf stick and let him or her choose a position at some number on the clock face. The winner was the one who "holed out" in the smallest number of strokes.

After this, everyone except one of the girls seated themselves in a circle. This one girl left the room. While she was gone someone paid her a compliment. Upon her return to the room, Jane told her, "Mary, someone has said that you were a very excellent skipper. Who was it?" Mary had three guesses to learn the identity of her admirer. If she guessed correctly, that one left the room. If she didn't guess her admirer, she chose someone else to leave. After this game of "Compliments," the club members had a good old songfest, remembering particularly the songs they had sung together last summer on the beach.

At going-home time it was almost hard to remember to don storm coats and galoshes, the illusion of a summer beach party had been so strong.

MIDSUMMER SNOW PARTY

"To think I ever kicked about winter weather."
Jean sat in the shade fanning herself lazily. "I
just haven't pep enough to even think."

"Oh, forget the heat," laughed Nancy. "It could be
worse. Besides we've got to plan a party for the crowd. It's
our turn to entertain."

Jean looked at Nancy disgustedly. "I suppose you want
me to dream about snow drifts and ice."

Nancy looked thoughtful. "I believe you've got something there. Let's give a snow party!"

"In July!" exclaimed Jean. And after a moment—"It'd
be different."

Thus it came about that Nancy and Jean had the crowd
in for a July snow party.

The invitations were cut from white cardboard to represent a snowman. Colored crayons marked the features
and round black buttons down the front of his coat. Between the buttons was this invitation:

> Come cool off
> At our snow party
> July 8, at 7 P.M.
> Jean and Nancy.

In preparation for the party the girls hung myriads of
sparkling snowflakes from the ceiling of the living room

and stuck large ones a foot in diameter on the walls. (The snowflakes were made from folded paper cut many times, dotted and smeared with glue and then sprinkled with metallic flakes.) They were hung with threads, then Scotch-taped to the ceiling. At the front door stood an enormous thermometer indicating below zero. Electric fans created a breeze from every corner of the room.

Their invitation backfired on the girls, however, for when the night of the party came, although it was a sizzling hot evening, the guests arrived wearing ear muffs, mittens, scarves, and galoshes. Even their sense of humor couldn't force them into winter coats.

Of course, this bit of horse-play started the evening off with hilarity. As soon as the guests had doffed their winter accessories, which we guarantee they did quickly, the girls passed out squares of white tissue paper, and told the crowd the best snowflakes would win a prize. Fortunately for the crowd, some of them remembered way back when they used to fold a square of tissue first into halves, then quarters, and then eighths and then proceed to snip off here and there a corner of the folded tissue. When unfolded, the result looked like an intricate snowflake pattern. It was fascinating to do on a hot night, and soon each individual had four or five unusual snowflakes to his credit. The girls then handed out sheets of colored construction paper on which to stick the flakes. The winner was awarded a snowball.

This snowball was an apple wrapped in cotton and tied with a red ribbon at the stem. When the crowd put up a howl that they were being cheated and that their snowflakes were superior to the winner's, Nancy gave each of the guests a snowball apple. She had intended to anyway.

For the next game the girls had torn off the monthly sheets of an old calendar—large size. On each sheet they had crossed off fifteen or sixteen different days so that each sheet had fifteen days remaining. Then they cut another month into individual dates which they put into a box. Before starting this game the girls passed out small favors to each guest. Each package was wrapped in Christmas paper and tied with fancy ribbon. The boys got combs, key chains, and pencils. The girls received bows, bobby pins, and combs. When the presents were undone they were laid in a row on the table.

Jean then handed out navy beans to be used as markers. The game then proceeded like bingo. When Nancy drew a number from the box, everyone having that number on his calendar (the crossed-out ones didn't count) put a bean on it. The first one to have all the numbers on his sheet covered sang out "Snowman." He then was permitted to take his choice of all the favors on the table, regardless of ownership. Of course, this created a great deal of joshing, but every man had his turn until all the gifts were disposed of.

After this hilarious game, the crowd divided into two teams and the girls brought out two storm windows covered with frost (Bon Ami). One window stood in the living room, the other in the adjoining dining room. A captain from each team left the room, and both were told to draw in the frost on the window the same picture, without telling what they were drawing. Each team had to guess what picture its captain was drawing. The team guessing first was the winner.

The first picture to be drawn was that of a sleigh; second, a boy sliding down hill; the third was to depict "Snowbound." The game was fascinating, as none of these young people were artists—which made it all the funnier. After one team had won three times straight, the other team insisted on a change of captains, which started the game off anew.

At this time a game of "Ice" was the order of the day.

The girls handed out slips of paper with questions on them to be answered with a word containing ice. Some of the questions were:

Answers

1. A 4-letter ice the world would be better
   without . . . .   Vice
2. A 6-letter ice that occurs three times   Thrice
3. A 5-letter ice fixed by the merchant .   Price
4. A dainty four-letter ice . . . . .   Nice
5. A 4-letter ice feared by the gals . .   Mice
6. A 5-letter ice that is cut . . . .   Slice
7. A 5-letter ice used in pickles . . .   Spice
8. A 5-letter ice that repeats itself . . . Twice
9. A 4-letter ice seen at weddings . . .   Rice
10. A 6-letter ice that is easier to give than
    to take . . . .   Advice

The dining-room table carried out the same winter scene. The centerpiece was a wreath of small pine branches, tied with silver bows and decorated with bright-colored Christmas-tree balls and large pine cones. Tall red candles added the grand touch. All the refreshments were served buffet style, with a sprig of fir tied with a red bow on each tray. Tuna-fish salad with hot buns, and iced tea, and for dessert snowballs of ice cream and cookies with frosting snowman faces completed the meal.

The guests claimed they had actually forgotten the heat in the chilly party and donned ear muffs and galoshes before saying a warm farewell.

Party Fun for
Special Days

BARBARA'S VALENTINE BEE

"I wish I had lots of brothers and sisters to make valentines with me." Barbara pushed her braids back over her shoulders as she sat on the floor, her "valentine makings" spread out before her.

"Next best to lots of brothers and sisters is lots of friends, Barbara," answered her mother. "How would you like to give a Valentine Bee?"

"What's that?" Barbara was immediately interested.

"Well, it would be sort of a valentine party where you and your friends could make your valentines together."

Plans were immediately under way. Barbara made a fold of red construction paper and cut it heart shape. When it was opened up it read:

> Be my Valentine
> At my Valentine Bee
> Tuesday, February 14
> At three P.M.
> Barbara.

Before the day of the party Barbara and her mother laid in a supply of valentine makings which consisted of several packages of red and white construction paper, a number of packages of lacy paper doilies, the small size, and some library paste. In addition she ransacked the attic for left-over lengths of wallpaper with floral designs.

She also cut out of old magazines a supply of cute dog and cat pictures.

When the guests arrived they found these makings spread out on card tables arranged so that four children could work at each table. In addition to the makings each table was supplied with scissors and plenty of crayons.

The children were soon at work. Some pasted pictures on squares of red construction paper. Lacy frills cut from the paper doilies pasted around the picture made a pretty frame.

One ambitious youngster drew a picture in the center of a red heart, then made a lace frame stand out by pasting one end of a two-inch long narrow strip of cardboard to each side of her red heart. Then she made a couple of folds in the strip and pasted the other end to the lacy frame.

The completed valentines were lined up on the mantel and the children chose the prettiest, the funniest, the fanciest, and the cleverest.

After this bit of quiet work the youngsters were glad for a lively game. Barbara divided the guests into two groups of equal number. The groups stood on opposite sides of the room. Barbara gave the first in each line an envelope containing three valentines, each of which bore a four-line verse. When Barbara gave the signal for the game to start, the leader at the head of the line took the valentines out of the envelope one by one, read them aloud, put them back in the envelope and handed the envelope to the next player. As both lines read valentines aloud at the same time, the noise was hilarious. The first line to get the valentines read all the way down the line won the game.

The next game was a valentine "Heart Hunt" with a different twist. Beforehand Barbara's mother had hidden dozens of small red hearts made of construction paper, in every conceivable place around the house. The children paired off in teams and joined hands. The hunt began while Barbara's mother played the piano. They hunted fast and furious, as long as the music continued. When the music stopped they stopped in their tracks. If anyone moved after the music stopped or if he dropped his partner's hands while hunting, he was disqualified. The team finding the most hearts won the game.

After the excitement of the "Heart Hunt" Barbara passed out a dozen candy hearts to each guest—the kind that bears a sentimental or slang expression. She offered a prize to the one making the most complete sentence from the words on the hearts. Some fast trading of hearts went on, as the youngsters tried to get candies with expressions that would fit together. This game proved to be very lively entertainment.

For the next game the group was divided into two teams. Each team formed a circle. In the center of each circle Barbara put a large pie tin on the floor. Then she passed to each a paper plate for a fan. In the one circle she sprinkled red tissue-paper hearts all over the floor. In the other circle she used white tissue-paper hearts. At a signal everyone started fanning with the plate, trying to blow the hearts into the pie tins. This game was very hilarious because the harder the fanning the higher the hearts flew. And they blew out of the pie tin almost easier than they blew in. The team with the most hearts in the pan after ten windy minutes won the game.

In the wide arched doorway between the living and dining room Barbara's mother hung about a foot apart a number of red cardboard hearts from strings of varying length. One at a time, each guest was blindfolded, given a pair of scissors, turned around three times and told to snip a heart. Then her partner of the "Heart Hunt" game held a short piece of string the end of which was fastened around the blinded guest's wrist. The partner could say nothing, but tried to guide his partner toward the hearts with small tugs at the string. The team snipping down the most hearts won the game.

The youngsters were fascinated with the valentine supper which concluded the party. Pink ham decorated with white potato-salad heart, and heart-shaped red Jello salad carried out the color scheme. White heart-shaped sandwiches and tall glasses of milk added the filling. Dessert was a brick of white ice cream with molded pink hearts in the center.

After the party Barbara agreed with her mother that next best to lots of brothers and sisters were lots of friends for making valentines.

SALLY'S VALENTINE PARTY

Sally was delighted that her turn to entertain "the club" fell near Valentine's Day because "it's so easy to give a party with a valentine theme."

Because glamour is super with the teeners, Sally was given free reign to make her party as pretty as possible. Her invitations were in the form of valentines made by cutting bright red construction paper four by six inches and folding down the middle to make a leaflet. On the outside of each folder she sketched a roguish little face and framed it with lacy bits cut from paper doilies. Of course, if she had preferred she could have cut faces from old magazines. The inside of the folder carried the following invitation:

> Will you be my Valentine
> on Friday next
> For a six o'clock supper?
> 805 Blunt Street.

Arriving guests soon decided that Dan Cupid must have planned and executed the decorations. Mirrors displayed bright red hearts. In some cases they formed frames; on others various designs. Scotch tape was used to stick them to the mirrors. If you have never tried this idea you will be surprised at its effectiveness. Red hearts also decorated the drapes, and red paper covers over

each lamp shade cast a rosy glow over the entire surroundings.

For the dining table a paper valentine cloth, bought at
the dime store, was perfect. The centerpiece looked like
a tree of tiny red hearts. Sally had dipped several bare
barberry branches in white paint. Each little thorn was
tipped with a bright red gumdrop. Sally at the time of
her party was unable to get the small red gumdrops so she
cut the larger ones into small pieces.

Each place card was a small white envelope bearing the
guest's name and decorated with tiny red paper hearts.
Regardless of the curiosity of the guests as to the contents
of the envelopes Sally insisted that they wait until they
had finished eating before opening them.

The supper itself was a valentine. Each plate contained
one large valentine which nearly filled the plate. The
effect was most intriguing. On closer inspection it was
discovered that the face of each valentine was half a hard-
boiled egg with the white rounding side up. Her lips were
two tiny strips of pimento, her eyes were raisins, her
nose a clove and the yellow curls were cheese shavings.
Her body was half an inverted peach pickle with three
clove buttons down the front of her waist. Her arms were
dainty white sticks of celery, cleverly snipped at the ends
for fingers. Her skirt, a large billowy lettuce leaf, concealed a generous helping of creamed chicken. Rolls and
milk completed the main course. Slices of angel food cake
topped with individual hearts of red ice cream completed
not only a delicious luncheon but one of strong eye appeal.

Supper over, the envelopes were opened. Each contained
red heart stickers, narrow strips of colored paper, figures
of Cupid and various other bits which Sally had cut from
old valentines. This little store of supplies was supple-

mented by sheets of red and white construction paper, a box of crayons, a jar of library paste, and scissors. Each guest was requested to make a valentine, from her supply, for a boy friend. Any style was permissible; pretty, fancy, or the old-style comic. This valentine-making was conducive to much jesting, commotion and comparing of notes. Rhymesters added clever verses while others printed their messages in prose. Prizes were awarded for the prettiest, the cleverest, and the funniest. The finished valentines were displayed on the mantel.

Next Sally asked each guest to write an adjective on the back of the envelope which bore her name. She collected the envelopes and then read a valentine romance which she had prepared beforehand using her guests as characters in the story. As she came to each name she preceded it by the adjective selected by that unsuspecting guest. For instance in the story "————— Mary Brown went walking one day and whom should she see but ————— Helen Grayson." Filling in the blanks with the adjectives each guest herself had chosen the story reads: "*Vicious* Mary Brown went walking one day and whom should she see but *gangling* Helen Grayson." This game was particularly funny because much of the time the unwitting guest had chosen an adjective most inappropriate; the fat guest choosing "skinny" and the like.

The next game was played on the dining-room table, which in the meantime was cleared for action. Each of six small dime-store blocks bore on each of its six faces, one of the letters H, E, A, R, T, S. The players took turns in rolling all the cubes at one throw. Each player kept her own score, giving herself one point for each word that could be made from the letters that came up. No letter could be used more than once, but it wasn't necessary to use all the letters each time. For example, when H, A, A, S, E, T came up, the thrower received nine points because she could make the nine words, "as," "tea," "hat," "sat," "set," "has," "heat," "the," and "ash." Ten points were scored if "hearts" could be spelled.

The result of the next game was surprising. This party included only a group who were very well acquainted. Each guest was given four cards; a blue, a gray, a green, and a brown. On the blue card each was asked to write the names of all the blue-eyed persons present; list the brown-eyed on the brown card; the gray-eyed on the gray; and the green-eyed on the green. The girls were very much chagrined to find that so many of them did not know the color of their friends' eyes. This precipitated a lot of joshing as to each other's lack of observation.

As the party broke up, the girls congratulated Sally on her many original party ideas.

WASHINGTON TEA PARTY

Last February Helen wanted to entertain her crowd. After considerable thought she decided on a Washington tea party. That type of party offered many and varied ideas for decorating and entertainment. Then too her school had a holiday on the 22nd of February which made it a perfect day for a party.

She printed her invitation on small cardboard hatchets which she cut from heavy construction paper. They read:

> Come over on Thursday
> At three P.M. to help
> Cut down the Cherry tree.
>   Helen.

Naturally her guests were much intrigued. They speculated as to whether or not they were supposed to really cut down a cherry tree. However, when the guests arrived they learned that this was an entirely different cherry tree from the one George Washington had chopped down. The cherry tree turned out to be a good-sized branch of barberry which of course at this time of year was bare. A flower holder in the bottom of an old-fashioned jardiniere held it upright. To keep it from tipping sidewise the jardiniere was filled with clean white sand.

The leaves and cherries on this tree were cut from construction paper and fastened to the tree by placing them on the tiny barberry thorns. The tree was very attractive and held a prominent place in the center of the living room.

But this tree was more than decoration—it started off the fun. Each girl was directed to take her turn in choosing a leaf from the tree. When the first girl had made her choice she discovered written on the back of her leaf an easy historical question such as "Name two famous men who had birthdays in February." If she could answer the question correctly she had a second choice. If she preferred to choose a cherry she could do so. But here was the joker. Some of the cherries were blank on the back, others bore this sentence, "I did it with my little hatchet." If her cherry was a blank she could then draw another leaf. But if her cherry had a sentence on the back she was required to do a stunt for the crowd—sing a song, turn a handspring, tell a story, or what have you. She could make her own choice.'

In this game the winner was the gal who had answered correctly the greatest number of historical questions. It was her privilege to impose forfeits in the way of stunts on the rest of the girls.

The next game smacked of the familiar "Donkey and His Tail" of earlier childhood parties, but was quite a grown-up version. On the wall Helen had taped a map of the United States. Then each guest was given an American Flag sticker on which she put her own initials.

The girls then took turns being blindfolded and trying to stick their flags on Washington, D. C. The one whose flag landed nearest its goal received a sack of candied cherries as a prize.

A "Cherry Race" was next in order. The guests were divided into two groups and assembled in two lines. The first in each line was given three large cherries. At a given signal each leader started across the room balancing the three cherries on the back of his left hand. If a cherry or two rolled off, the contestant had to pick them up unassisted and continue. When the leader reached the other side of the room he returned to his original place and gave the cherries to the next in line to continue the race. The team finishing first won the relay.

For the next game Helen used folding chairs because they were portable. The girls paired off in couples. All the couples but one seated themselves in a group. The remaining couple became George and Martha Washington. Each of the other couples secretly decided on a fruit to be their name. George and Martha wandered around the room calling out the names of various fruits such as cherries, apples, and pears. If a couple's fruit name was called they left their chairs and followed after George and Martha. If George or Martha called out, "The fruit trees are all in bloom," everyone left his seat and followed the Washingtons. When George called, "The fruit is all ripe," everyone dashed for a chair. The two not getting chairs became George and Martha for the next try.

After this bit of riotous exercise a quieter game was welcome. Helen put a large glass bowl in the center of a card table. She placed nearby a bunch of cotton balls which she claimed were white cherries. Each girl in turn was then blindfolded, turned around three times and given a wooden spoon. The object was to spoon the white cherries into the glass bowl. (Try it sometime. You'll have a surprise.) Because the cherries have no weight it is impossible to tell whether the spoon is empty or full, and not being able to see the bowl makes this game a real effort for the contestant, but very, very funny for the sidelines.

Place cards of paper hatchets proudly sporting bright red bows around a small cherry tree centerpiece—similar to the larger one that started off the party—made a gay refreshment table.

Generous slices of cherry pie topped with ice cream in hatchet mold brought the happy party to a close. The guests really enjoyed the Washington Tea Party.

ST. PATRICK'S DAY PARTY

Sure, 'tis a fine time to give a party—St. Patrick's Day. Make it a family party—invite the Caseys, the McCarthys, the Flanagans, and the O'Tooles. Include the Smiths and the Joneses, for we know, no matter what the name of your friends they will enjoy this type of fun.

Decorations are no problem—with plenty of green and white tissue to cover the lights, and decorate the table. Don't neglect clay pipes and shamrocks in your decoration scheme.

Invitations need be only simple little notes printed on green shamrocks:

> 'Tis St. Patrick's Day
> We're celebrating
> 'Tis the wearing of the Green
> You'll not be forgetting
> March 17th, 7 P.M.

Meet your guests at the door with a big green top hat filled with numbers. This hat can be made of cardboard, or an ordinary hat can be covered with green crepe paper. Let each arriving guest draw a number from the hat—green for the males and white for the women and girls with corresponding numbers.

When everyone has arrived you are all set for a bit of Irish blarney. The host or hostess calls out a man's num-

ber. He then proceeds to blarney his unknown partner
by telling her, among other things, what he considers the
loveliest thing about her. When he has finished his blarney the much complimented lady steps to his side.

Another number is called who in no uncertain words
expresses his admiration for the "willowy slenderness" of
his partner. When his corresponding number steps out
they are greeted with shouts of laughter. She turns out to
be the chunky young neighbor girl next door.

Keeping their partners, the entire group, with the exception of one person, forms a circle—males to the left of
the girls. This one person takes her place in the center of
the circle. Everybody marches to the following words (tune:
"We Won't Be Home Until Morning"):

> Got a pig in the parlor
> Got a pig in the parlor
> Got a pig in the parlor,
> And he is Irish too
> And he is Irish too
> And he is Irish too,
> Got a pig in the parlor
> Got a pig in the parlor
> Got a pig in the parlor
> And he is Irish too.

The ladies continue marching in the direction in which
they are going while the men turn about and go in the
other direction. When this change is made the "pig"
from the center joins the circle. The leader blows the whistle, and there is a scramble for new partners. One is bound
to be left out and he now becomes the "pig." After several
scrambles for partners the ice is pretty well broken and
the whistle sounds for change of game.

Arrange your guests into family groups, lending a child
here or there to make the groups equal in number. Then
introduce them to "Irish Golf." Each family is given a

large bowl, an Irish potato and a tablespoon. The object is to scoop the potato into the bowl with the spoon without lifting it from the table.

Add the strokes it takes each member of the family to get the potato into the bowl. To the winning family who accomplishes it with the least number of strokes goes an Irish potato.

Who ever heard of a St. Patrick's party without noise. Line up your family groups and provide each of them with a No. 10 paper bag. Let each family name a person for its goalee. The goalee stands across the room. At the whistle the first person in each family group line blows up his bag, runs to the family goalee, bursts the bag on the goal keeper's back, quickly returns to the line and touches off No. 2. The line finishing first is winner.

Next let the crazy Irish have a "Crazy Cane Race." Divide your guests into two groups of equal number. Give the first one in each group a cane. At the starting signal he is supposed to put his forehead on the top of the cane, and keep it there without moving the cane until he sidesteps six times around in a circle, counting each time he completes a circle. At the finish of the sixth round, ask him to walk to the opposite end of the room, touch a designated spot on the wall. Then turn around and return to the starting point and touch the next contestant in line. This does not sound like such a hilarious game, but all the contestants, being slightly dizzy, will have a terrific time walking in a straight line across the room and back. The game continues until one team finishes first.

After so much excitement, let each family form its own group. Allow five or ten minutes for each family to plan a yarn about a fishing or hunting trip or some adventure. At the end of the allotted time let the guests reassemble in one big group. When the competition starts, one member of the Jones family begins his yarn. The next mem-

ber of the family may add to it, and so on, until the family
has all helped or the allotted five minutes is up, which-
ever comes first. This is a thrilling experience for the
younger members of the family.

After each family has spun its tale, three judges, previously appointed, will decide which yarn was the best,
which the cleverest, and which one the funniest. A bag of
green and white candy may be awarded the family with
the best all-around story.

The Irish like to eat and since all your guests are Irish,
at least for this party, serve a hearty lunch. A steaming
Irish stew, a green-tinted grapefruit salad, and hard rolls
will bring out the blarney in your guests. Complete the
meal with green mint sundaes and limeade. Surely 'twill
be an Irish party that'll long be remembered with words
of praise that are not blarney.

AN "APRIL FOOL"
DINNER PARTY

With a family of children April Fool's Day can be one big headache or it can be fun for everyone—depending a lot on how you take it. There is nothing gradester-age children love better than playing tricks and April Fool's Day is the day of opportunity for such activities.

The spirit of the day is an excuse (if you ever need one) for a party. It's bound to be fun because everyone is specially geared for fun on that day. Let your youngsters invite in their friends for a dinner party—it won't be formal, but we'll guarantee it'll be exciting.

Written invitations seem to whet the edge of anticipation. For such invitations our youngsters used small white cards on which they wrote:

> Dinner at Six on April Fool's Day
> After which comes an evening of play.
> Come—Be amazed and curious
> For fun will grow fast and furious.

Promptly at six o'clock all the guests arrived in their best "bib and tucker." We had gone all out to make the dinner table look as pretty and partyish as any grown-up's party with lace tablecloth, best china and gleaming silver. Spring colors, pink, lavender and green were in evidence in candles and the sweet-pea centerpiece. Paper drinking-cups and paper napkins in the same soft pastel colors added to the beauty of the table without striking an odd note. It was lovely to look at and there was nothing to indicate that things were not what they seemed.

Mary was the first guest to run into trouble. She took a drink of water, and immediately with a chagrined look around dabbed at the water on her chin.

Teddy wasn't so reticent. After a couple of drinks he burst out, "What's the matter with me tonight? I can't drink without spilling."

"Hey, there's something the matter with these cups." On the quiet Johnny had been looking his cup over. Examination proved that every third or fourth cup was a dribble cup. (A dribble cup is one with small holes about an inch from the top out of which water leaks when the cup is put to the lips.)

Now the youngsters were on the alert for April Fool tricks, but it didn't lessen their appetites. Chicken and dumplings, fruit salad, and new peas disappeared like magic, but not without a hitch or two.

Sally was embarrassed when her fork broke just above the tines as she tried to spear a bit of chicken. With many cautions about care of silver she was given another which broke in the same way. Then someone tumbled that these were trick forks.

A moment later everyone was startled by what sounded like the explosion of a firecracker. It was a trick knife that exploded when Hank started to use it.

Suddenly and with no reason at all a candle went out. In a few minutes out went another, to be followed by others at short intervals. In a very short time the table was in darkness. As soon as possible we relighted the candles and the meal progressed.

When Ruth discovered a big spider on the sweet peas

the girls were horrified. It turned out to be a fake as were the crickets which filled the sugar bowl. When Teddy passed the pickle dish a huge butterfly flew from under it and sailed across the table. Of course, the boys had to retrieve the butterfly and examine it and then try it again and again.

All these paper novelties are inexpensive and can be purchased at any novelty shop. The trick with the candles was simple. Cut a candle clear across through the wick any distance you wish from the top, depending on how long you want it to burn. Then heat the severed parts and press wax together. The cut is not then noticeable. The candle will burn until it gets down to the cut wick when it goes out.

By the time the dessert of upside-down cake—an appropriate April Fool's Day dessert—had been devoured, these young moderns were ready for an evening of fun. They were much intrigued with that very appropriate April Fool game of "I Doubt It."

There were eight youngsters. We used two decks of playing cards shuffled together. The cards were all dealt around the table. The object of the game is to get rid of one's cards.

The first person playing starts with ones or aces. He picks a given number of cards from his hand and says, laying them face down in the center of the table, "I am playing three aces." If he looks honest and you think he is playing just three cards and they are aces, no one "doubts it." The next person in line plays twos, the third threes, etc. At any time anyone playing may "doubt" the honesty of the player. If the player has misstated his play and someone "doubts" it, the player takes the whole pile of cards which has accumulated in the center of the table. If he has stated his play correctly, the doubter takes the whole pile. If it is the player's turn to play fours and he does not have any, he substitutes something else and still announces he is playing fours. Perhaps he will get by with it and perhaps his bluff will be called by a "doubter."

The winner gets a prize and the loser (the one with the most cards in his hands when the game is finished) gets a dunce's cap.

This game turned out to be so interesting that the evening was gone and it was time to go home before anyone realized it. The youngsters declared the party had been the most fun of any April Fool party they could remember. As they left for their homes they were still trying to get "April Fool" on each other.

AN "EGGCITING" EASTER PARTY!

"The guys'll think I've holes in my head, if I ask them over for an Easter Egg Hunt." Sandy brushed a lock of his stubborn red hair back with grimy fingers.

I sighed as I watched him. He certainly had outgrown the adorable stage when he delighted to celebrate his April birthday by having his friends over for an Easter Egg Hunt. But in spite of his long legs and grimy appearance he still wanted a birthday party.

"Can't we think up something to do, Mom, that big fellows my age would like?"

I kept to myself the thought that eleven wasn't exactly old age. "Maybe we could have an Easter party and plan some different games."

"I know, Mom! Let's have an egg party. Egg eats, egg games, egg stunts, egg everything."

"Eggs, son? That sounds awfully—well eggy. But make your plans and I'll help."

When he first outlined his ideas to me, I thought, "That party will take so many eggs it may be rather expensive." But when I realized that the only expense for the games and decorations would be the cost of the eggs used, I decided that it would really be an inexpensive party. Thus it came about that Sandy gave an egg party on Easter Monday, his birthday.

He cut the egg-shaped invitations from colored construction paper. The invitations read, "Come to Sandy's house on Monday at *eggsactly* 3 P.M. for an *eggciting* afternoon." Then off he dashed on his bicycle to deliver his invitations.

Promptly on the hour eleven well-scrubbed boys arrived, eager for anything that sounded like fun. Just in case an April shower might chase us into the house later in the afternoon we staged our egg-catching contest first. That was the only one of our planned games that could not be played in the house.

The game goes this way: Six boys, each with a raw egg, line up faced by a partner. Each of the six boys on one side tosses the egg in his possession to the boy facing him who stands three feet from him. If this boy catches the egg without breaking it, each boy takes a big step backwards. If the egg is not caught but smashes to the ground that couple is eliminated. After each throw each partner moves backward one step. You'll be surprised at what an exciting game this is, and how adept eleven-year-olds are at tossing and catching raw eggs. The two boys who finally won were made leaders in the "Egg Relay Race."

Two hard-boiled eggs were used for the relay. The two leaders took turns choosing team mates. The lads then formed two lines, the one boy directly behind the other. Every lad was given a teaspoon with instructions to hold the handle between his teeth. A hard-boiled egg was placed in the bowl of the spoon of each of the two leaders. At a signal the leaders, with their hands behind them, ran to a goal across the lawn without dropping the eggs. If the lad accomplished it he grabbed the spoon in his hand, ran back to the line and placed the egg in the spoon of the boy who stood just back of him in line.

If the egg was dropped in transit the boy carrying it picked it up, placed it back on the spoon before advancing farther. The team completing the race first was declared "Eggsperts."

Next on the agenda was an egg-cracking contest. Each contestant held an egg in his hand, small end up and challenged someone to crack his egg. The challenged lad then with his own egg tapped the egg of the challenger. If the challenged cracked the egg of the challenger he won the challenger's cracked egg. If his own was cracked he turned it over to the challenger. The boys continued to challenge one another until only one uncracked egg remained. The possessor of that egg was declared "The Great Uncracked."

After so much activity the boys were perfectly willing to sit down while each peeled his cracked egg ready for the next stunt. This stunt is not new, but it's always fun and surprising for each new group that tries it. Each boy is given an empty milk bottle, clean of course, with the request that he put the egg into his bottle. The peeled egg is larger than the top of the bottle. The boys pushed and squeezed on the slippery eggs but made no progress. Sandy produced a match and showed his friends the trick. He dropped a lighted match into the bottle. He placed the egg on the mouth of the empty bottle and they all watched the egg slide into the bottle. It was not long until each bottle contained an egg. One thoughtful youngster wanted to know why.

Sandy explained that the lighted match in the bottle used up the oxygen in the bottle thereby creating a partial vacuum. Then the outside air pressure forces the egg into the bottle.

To get the eggs out of the bottles was something else again. With all the shaking, jiggling, and jouncing the eggs would not come. Sandy very nonchalantly claimed it was very simple. He just turned the bottle upside down and blew into it, and the pressure of air then forced the egg out of the bottle. The lads were delighted with their know-how and were promising themselves a lot of fun outwitting their own families.

By this time we were ready to call the boys for eats— the likes of which is not usually considered birthday-party fare. But it was in accordance with Sandy's idea and made a hit with the gang.

Scrambled eggs and bacon with slices of buttered brown bread and tall glasses of milk disappeared in unbelievably short order. The birthday cake was decorated with candy Easter eggs stuck in the frosting.

In saying Good-bye the lads assured Sandy his party had been an *Eggciting* affair.

CELEBRATE THE
FOURTH OF JULY

Siss, Boom, Bah! The Fourth of July, Hurrah! That's the spirit of the day that we all used to celebrate with a great banging of fireworks from dawn until nightfall or until we ran out of firecrackers. In most states this dangerous sort of Fourth of July fun has been banned because of the high casualty lists.

But no laws or ordinances have put a ban on fun, so what to do on the Fourth of July? Why not invite the girls and boys over for a Picnic Party on your lawn—the weather's apt to be clear and hot, the enthusiasm of the guests will run high, and there'll be no casualty list to mar the fun.

An excellent starter for this yard picnic could be "Find the Flag." Send one of your guests into the house. Someplace in the yard hide an American flag, so that the entire crowd except the absent member knows where it is. Call back the hunter and explain to him that while he hunts the flag the crowd is going to sing "Yankee Doodle" —softly when he is far from it, louder as he nears it, and very loud when he gets it. This is a jolly game that youngsters love—each one will want his turn at finding the flag.

For real exertion introduce a "Backward Relay." Divide the guests into two groups of equal number. Get

about two dozen rolled-up newspapers and lay them on
the ground in two rows. The rows should be about eight
feet apart and the newpapers should be laid at intervals
of about two feet. Contestants must hop backward over
the newspapers to the goal and return. When the first
player on each side returns, he touches off the next one.
The side which finishes first wins the relay. The excitement over this game will run high—and the noise will
equal that of firecracker days.

By this time the players will be glad to relax a bit. The
guests are seated in a circle for the game of "Face." The
first player turns to the one on his right and says, "You
have a face," to which the other replies, "What kind of
face?" The first player then must answer with a descriptive adjective beginning with "a." He could say, "You
have an angelic face" or "an attractive face," or if he feels
funny he might say, "You have an awful face." The next
player turns to the one on his right and says, "You have a
face." The second player answers the inquiry "What kind
of a face?" with an adjective beginning with "b" and so on
around the circle and through the alphabet. The same
adjective cannot be used twice. Anyone who can't think of
an adjective beginning with the right letter before the
conductor counts to ten must leave the circle and sit in
the center while the others finish the game. The game
gets very exciting towards the close when only two or
three of the sharpest are left to seek new adjectives.

The great outdoors is the ideal place for this next game
which is a trifle wet. Put to float a large number of small
corks in a tub of water. It is well to use a tub or at least a
large dishpan so that the corks cannot be easily pushed
against the bottom. Give a contestant a pin and tell him
to spear as many corks as he can in three minutes. The
cork must not be touched by hand, neither may it touch
the sides of the pan while being harpooned.

If your party is large and your tub ample, two players can be spearing at the same time. But don't pass out pins to the players until they are ready for their turn at the tub, or some rascally lad will be sure to harpoon a guest or two.

In a free-for-all picnic spirit let "Bombs" be the next game. Once again divide your guests into two groups of equal number. Have the two teams line up facing each other, about eight or ten feet apart. Give each player a toy balloon and when the game starts, the player at the head of each line must inflate his balloon until it bursts. The next in line then does the same, and so on down the line. No cheating is allowed. The second player must wait to blow up his balloon until the first man's balloon has popped. The group first popping all its balloons wins. This breath-taking game provides plenty of noise to satisfy the most noise-thirsty.

By this time even the liveliest will be ready to sit down for a quiet game. Provide each one with a card and pencil and announce that ten minutes will be allowed for the players to list as many states in the United States as they can. Even fairly young children are familiar with most of the states in the Union and will enjoy the contest. If your group is unusually sharp, ask them to list the capitals of each state.

During this brain-racking event, you will have an excellent opportunity to set out the picnic table. Truly American food will be welcome at this Picnic Party, especially if there is plenty of it. So bring on the hot dogs and toasted buns, a big bowl of potato salad, or potato chips for those who prefer them, pickles, and perhaps a casserole of hot baked beans. Finish off this menu with "pinwheel" cake, commonly recognized as a slice of jelly roll, and ice-cream cones.

SMALL FRY
HALLOWEEN PARTY

Do you have someone at your house who is "too big for a fairy, but too little for a man" — someone who just loves Halloween, yet is too young to go out "Trick-and-treating"?

If so, why not let him invite a few of his pre-school friends to a Halloween costume party. He'll thrill over dressing up and feel he's really a big boy now. This applies to little girls as well as boys.

It's much fun to decorate for Halloween because the traditional orange and black is so colorful, and stores are filled with inexpensive cut-outs that can be taped to windows, pinned on drapes, hung from chandeliers, and fastened to lamp shades.

We always cover our lamp shades with orange crepe paper, tied around the top edge with a strip of black paper and decorated here and there with black cut-outs. Such decorations give the room a real Halloween flavor.

If you want to use invitations, cut them from orange construction paper in the shape of a pumpkin. With black crayon draw a jack-o-lantern face on one side and on the other print the invitation.

> Come to Johnny's
> On Halloween day
> At four P. M.
> For a Costume Party.

When the youngsters gather — and we'll guarantee every one of them will be there — they will at first be completely occupied with examining each other's costumes. The chances are this will be the only costume party they have attended.

The first fun might be making Halloween paper weights. Beforehand collect four or five rocks, approximately paper-weight size — one for each guest. Scrub each rock well and draw on it with a pencil a jack-o-lantern face. Give each child a supply of crayons and a rock. Let him color the rock to his liking. If he doesn't stay within the lines, it doesn't really matter. The important thing to him is that he will be creating a jack-o-lantern paper weight he can proudly take home.

After this bit of concentration, these young witches and goblins will be ready for a familiar activity such as blowing soap bubbles. This requires an old-fashioned clay pipe (one for each child, please), two-thirds of a quart of soapy water, a teaspoonful of sugar and four tablespoonfuls of glycerine or vegetable oil for durable bubbles. No need to assure you that this part of the fun will be a success. All youngsters love to blow bubbles.

Small youngsters always enjoy a wishing well. Beforehand make a "well" out of heavy paper and decorate it with Halloween figures. Give each youngster a fishing stick with a string on it. To each line as it is dropped attach a small gayly-wrapped package. The youngsters will enjoy unwrapping the bundle to find some little toy such as a doll or horn or funny hat. For this age group all the toys should be the same. In that way everyone is satisfied.

Frequently little children seem to find tremendous fascination about a game that proceeds entirely in silence. It is called a Beckoning game. The children stand in a circle. One child in the center is "IT." "IT" beckons to a child in the ring. The child beckoned to comes into the center, shakes hands with "IT" and repeats the action of the first youngster. Game continues until each child has been beckoned to.

Because late refreshments spoil a youngster's appetite for supper, it is much better to serve a light meal at five-thirty. A Halloween tablecloth and Halloween

paper plates and cups make a bright festive table for
the little masqueraders. All kidfolk love amusing foods
so serve a Hamburger Jack-o-lantern. Decorate the hamburger with green pepper eyebrows, stuffed olive eyes,
carrot strip nose and mouth. Serve him on a big bun.
Put vegetable soup in a Halloween cup and serve another cupful of milk. For dessert a scoop of chocolate
ice cream, with marshmallow features and an ice cream
cone hat will tickle their imaginations as well as their
palates.

Half the fun of "trick-and-treating" is having a sack
of goodies to look over and sample the next day. Give
each guest a small sack. Let each one go around the
room and take a "treat" from dishes placed at strategic
spots.

With their sacks of Halloween "loot," jack-o-lantern
paperweights, small wishing well toys, and soap bubble
pipes, the little masqueraders will have a party to talk
about for days on end.

KIDDIE-CAT PROWL

Halloween — what a night for cats! Let's have a party for prowling cats, leering cats, purring cats and snarling cats. With paper cats pinned on curtains and taped to lampshades. And kiddie-cats. A kiddie-cat is you, wearing a cat costume your mother can make.

Half the guests are asked to come in orange cat costumes, half to wear black. Dad and Mom wear masks to match your costume. You'll follow paper cat paw prints into your host's home — orange ones lead to girls' coat room, black ones lead to boys'. Then the cat frolic begins.

Does a cat always land on its feet? Not this one. It's paper, with one orange side and one black. Orange cats form one line, black cats another. Your host throws the paper cat in the air. If it lands orange side up, orange cats laugh. Black cats look glum. If it lands black side up, black cats laugh. You must join the opposite line if you laugh out of turn. After five throws, longest line wins. Host awards each winner a black pipe-cleaner "whisker" to tape on his face.

Next, kiddie-cats show milk-lapping talents. Each gets a saucer of milk. Black cats crouch together, opposite orange cats. At the word "Meow," you start lapping. (Did you ever lap milk? It's pretty funny.) The team that licks saucers clean first, wins and gets whiskers.

For the Cat Grinning Game, cats form a circle. They must stay sober until the host points at one. That cat grins like a Cheshire, wipes the grin off and throws it across the circle to a friend. The friend grabs the grin, spread it on his face and smiles broadly. Toss grin back and forth. If you smile out of turn, you're out. Ousted cats leer to make players laugh. Last three sober-sides get whiskers.

"Cat on the Back Fence" tests alley cats' skill. Cats pussyfoot backwards on all fours on tape "fences" pinned to the carpet. Each team has a fence. You keep feet and hands on the "fence" all the way and meow. Most nimble team wins a whisker for each member.

It's whisker-counting time! Cats with the most get black gum-drop cats with candy-corn eyes. Others get orange cats with licorice eyes.

Then all leering cats, purring cats, snarling cats and alley cats feast on doughnuts and cider. And you all prowl homeward.

DOROTHY'S HALLOWEEN
PARTY

"Oh, Joyce, isn't this a cute invitation to Dorothy's Halloween party? Is yours just like it?" asked Ruth.

"Let's see," said Joyce. "Mine says:

> This is the tail of the Halloween cat
> Hurry, he says, to meet Witch and Bat
> On Halloween Eve, about 7 or so
> To a house that you all know.
> Bring some apples for a mysterious purpose."

"That's just like mine except that mine says to bring oranges," said Ruth. "Johnny told me that he had an invitation too but he was asked to bring canned goods and some of the boys were asked to bring candy. I wonder what it means. Maybe it's to be a picnic lunch."

"No-oo-oo, I don't believe that. But anyway it'll be fun because Dorothy always thinks of something different."

The great evening finally arrived. A tall spook met the guests at the door and collected their gifts of food. It was a very exciting spook because he grew shorter and shorter before their very eyes. Then just as he was a normal size his head shot way up in the air. Everyone wanted to know what made the spook change size, so Dorothy explained that John held a broom underneath a sheet. On top of the broom was the ghost's head, and as

John raised and lowered the broom the spook grew and shrank.

This hilarity was followed by a ghost story. The only light in the room was from four lighted candles. These were placed in the center of the room, guests around them in a circle. As the spooky ghost story proceeded the candles went out one at a time until the room was in darkness. No one could understand why the candles suddenly went out until Dorothy explained that the trick is to cut the candles in two and then stick them together again by heating them. When the candle burns down to the cut wick, naturally it goes out.

"How would you all like to be goblins and do a Halloween errand?" Dorothy asked.

"Do you mean ring doorbells and run?" asked Deane.

"There wouldn't be much fun in that if we didn't leave something, would there?" asked Dorothy. "Leaving something at the door on Halloween! That's a new one on me," exclaimed Joyce, "but it sounds like fun."

"You all know about that poor family with a bunch of small children living near the edge of town? Wouldn't it be fun," said Dorothy, "to put on masks, put all the food you brought into small baskets, put it on their doorstep, knock and run. We can hide and watch the fun when they find all the good things to eat."

"Swell idea." "What fun!" All the boys and girls were thrilled with the plan. Dorothy had masks for each guest. The food was loaded into the family car. As soon as Dorothy's Daddy was ready to drive they all piled in and were on their way.

When they reached the edge of town, they left the car. They were whispering and giggling as they approached the house with the food. They sneaked up to the door, deposited the baskets and sneaked away. Long-legged Deane was left to knock and then run.

The door opened and the mother stepped out. She stooped and looked into the baskets. Then she peered all around. Then she looked again in the baskets. She was very excited as she called to her family, "Come children and see what the Halloween witch has left us." Several small children came tumbling out, squealing with delight.

Dorothy and her goblin guests could hardly keep from shouting their laughter because the mother thought the Halloween witch had been there. "Deane is surely the witch," said Dorothy. "He knocked on the door."

Soon the whole happy crowd returned to Dorothy's house for refreshments. There were glasses of milk or cider, and doughnuts strung on the handle of a broom were passed. Deane, the witch, passed the doughnuts.

It was a gay bunch that bade their hostess Good Night, assuring her that it had been the best Halloween party ever.

BLACK CATS CELEBRATE

Halloween and parties go together like the horse and carriage. You never think of one without the other. Whether it is a "Goblin Party," a "Black Cat Party," a "Kilkenny Party," a "Witches' Festival," or a "Pumpkin Masquerade," the secret of a successful party depends upon preparation for it. The most successful parties always seem to be spontaneous and entirely unplanned, but invariably in the background is a wise host or hostess with a definite plan.

Of all the Halloween parties at our house, the Black Cat party stands out. We decorated everywhere with Black Cat cut-outs. We had prowling black cats, leering cats, sitting cats and snarling black cat cut-outs pinned to the drapes, taped to the mirrors and windows, and decorating the lamp shades. (We covered the lamp shades with orange crepe paper and then pasted the black cat cut-outs to the paper. With the lights on, the effect was most Halloweenish.)

Invitations were written in white ink on black cat cut-outs.

Black Cats Celebrate
Halloween night at seven
Come in costume
805 Blunt Street

Each guest upon arrival was given an envelope containing paper letters. These letters when placed in the right order spelled a cat's name such as "Pussy, Tabby,

Kitty, Fluff, Tiny, etc." As soon as each player figured out his cat's name, he wrote it on a slip of paper and pinned it on. When a plump "gal" turned out to be "Tiny" and a serious scholar became "Fluff," it broke the ice and the party was off to a good start.

For a lively game we divided our group into teams with six players each. Teams lined up for a walking-relay to reach the finishing line across the room. Each one of the six players on the team was given a handicap such as:

1st player — Cat has a sore front paw
2nd player — Cat has hurt his back paw
3rd player — Cat walks with arched back
4th player — Cat prowls
5th player — Cat bats at a ball as he goes
6th player — Cat washes face with paw as he travels.

The team doing everything correctly and having the sixth player cross the finishing line first, won the game.

Next we tried a Cat Fight. We drew a circle about eight feet in diameter (Chalk will vacuum off a carpet). Two players stood in the circle. They stooped and grasped their own ankles. At a signal each tried to push the other from the circle or out of balance — meowing all the while. A player lost when he left the circle, released either hand, or touched the ground with any part of his body except his feet.

Cat's Day is an excellent charade. Each guest received a slip of paper on which was typed a stunt similar to these.

Imitate a cat meeting a dog.
Imitate a cat licking its chops.
Imitate a cat howling on the back fence.
Imitate a cat in a cat fight.
Imitate a cat washing its face.
Imitate a cat sharpening its claws on a tree.
Imitate a cat greeting its master.

As each stunt was performed the rest tried to guess what the actor was doing.

Next the guests tried their hands at making funny cats. We placed a bowl of fruit, a dish of cloves, some black jelly beans, some pieces of yarn, a box of toothpicks and a pincushion of pins on a table. To start the fun off we suggested a cat with a lemon body — knob end for nose. Black-headed pins for eyes, a bunch of yarn for a tail and toothpicks for legs. The variety of possibilities is endless and the crowd was soon on its way with small cats, big cats, slick cats, fuzzy cats, and fat cats.

Refreshments can be as simple or as elaborate as you wish, but simple refreshments are always popular. We served pumpkin pie and cider. Each piece of pie was decorated with a cat made of whipped cream.

A HALLOWEEN TRAIL
OF TERROR

Another delightful Halloween party is a progressive Halloween party. The advantage of the house-to-house party is that youngsters can be out of doors part of the time which gives them active exercise that fulfills yearnings for a rip-roaring good time.

The young guests may be asked to come, masked, to Pumpkin-Face Inn. The address must be that of the first house on the trail. The guests upon their arrival are given a small sack of buttered corn and four crackers. Here each guest submits to the "Ghost Test" which consists of eating the four crackers and then whistling. Try it sometime and see what a feat it is. The first successful whistler is given a lollypop.

The group is then told that there are paper pumpkins hidden throughout the house. The guests are divided into four groups, each with a leader. Each leader is provided with a string on which to put the paper pumpkins when found. Each group chooses a signal such as barking, meowing or crowing. No one except the leader is allowed to pick up a pumpkin. When one of the others finds a pumpkin he places his finger on it and barks or meows or does whatever his group is supposed to do until the leader comes to pick it up. The group, whose leader has the longest string of pumpkins, wins. This game is very hilarious and youngsters love the noise that they can make while playing it.

The party then proceeds to the second house which is completely dark. An adult ghost (or two) accompanies the group from house to house. The second place is called Haunted House. The leader raps on the door three times; a ghost opens the door and instructs the guests to form a lock-step line and to follow him. Amid shrieks and groans the guests are led through the house and finally into a dimly lit room and told a ghost story.

After the ghost story the youngsters are provided with paper sacks, crayons and scissors with which to construct a mask. The best one is chosen by popular applause and the winner awarded a prize. Each youngster is then given a pocketful of peanuts and they all proceed to Witch's Cavern.

Here there is an old witch with a cauldron full of cookies and fortunes. The children are greatly delighted with the fortunes given them by the witch. They are then conducted to the kitchen of the home. Here apples bob in a tub full of water. Each child tries his luck at bobbing for apples. An apple is the reward for the guest who is able to rescue an apple from the water with his teeth. The one or two unsuccessful youngsters are then given apples before they proceed to the next house.

The Hideout is the last of the four houses. At the Hideout the guests are seated on the floor with a bowl of slippery pumpkin seeds in the center. Each child is given a needle and thread. At a given signal the children all begin to string the slippery pumpkin seeds. At the end of ten minutes a prize is given the youngster with the most seeds on his string.

Then the children are presented with a ball of Witch's Yarn. The first child unwinds the ball until he finds a slip of paper with his fortune on it. He then throws the ball to another child who unwinds until he finds his fortune, etc. Enough fortunes have been tied in the ball of yarn so that each guest will receive one.

The children are then served Halloween Sundaes. Halloween Sundaes are orange ice cream over which chocolate syrup is poured, topped off with imitation black spiders and chopped nuts.

The youngsters thoroughly enjoy this Halloween "Trail of Terror" party. Best of all it is not a great deal of work or expense for any one family, for the four families in the neighborhood who give the party share the work and expense. Perhaps you'd like to try this plan in your neighborhood.

A HARD-TIME
HALLOWEEN PARTY

Of the many different kinds of Halloween parties a hard-time party is bound to be intriguing.

Appropriate invitations for this type of party are written on torn pieces of brown paper decorated with a black-cat sticker. Black cats, witches, and bats from the dime store make effective home decorations. Pictures can be hung at an angle or upside down. The dressing table may boast a shiny pie tin used for a hand mirror along with an old comb minus many teeth. Gunny sacks make lovely window curtains for this hard-time affair.

Such a setting entails very little expense, not too much effort and creates an atmosphere of hilarity that starts the party off with a bang.

A game that all young people will enjoy is a game of "Halloween Ten Pins." This is especially good when bowling is so popular. In keeping with the hard-time motif use ginger ale bottles for pins and solid heads of cabbages for balls. Set a certain score for game and let some expert bowler keep score for the crowd. Don't keep at one game too long.

After this game "Match Box Relay" will be fun. Divide the guests into two teams, girls against boys. Let the hostess fasten the cover of a penny match box on the nose of each of the leaders. Each must transfer the box cover from his nose to the nose of the next team mate without the use of the hands. If the cover is dropped, it may be picked up and put back on the nose of the last person to have it. The team that finishes passing the box first is the winner, of course.

Halloween is synonymous with fortunetelling. No Halloween party would be complete without some sort of fortunetelling stunt, especially for teen-age youngsters. "Goblet Fortunes" are fun to do. Place a goblet on a table. Tie a ring to a string. Let each guest drop the ring to the bottom of the goblet while he recites the alphabet. Immediately when the ring strikes the side of the goblet the person stops. The letter with which he or she stops is indication of the name of the person he or she will marry.

"Halloween Hags" are lots of fun. Draw on a sheet a life-size witch with stringy hair, peaked hat, etc., with a hole where the face should be seen. Hang a sheet in an open doorway. Let the girls stick their heads in the opening, making faces to disguise their identities. Boys write their guesses as to who each one is. Then the girls take their turns at guessing whose face they see. It is surprising how hard it is to guess each face. The youngsters are very good at face-making and have a grand time doing it.

At the conclusion of the games serve your guests a hearty lunch. Have the dining table set with a clean ragged cloth or brown paper doilies. Cracked and nicked dishes are in order along with old and odd pieces of silverware. Candles stuck into empty pop bottles may be used for table lighting. Colored magazine ads that represent some fault or peculiarity of the guests may be used for place cards. This causes a riot of fun and you'd be surprised how quickly each guest will spot his place. Oyster stew, vegetable salad, rolls, pickles, jelly, pumpkin pie and cider will satisfy the hungriest guest and are not too hard to prepare.

HALLOWEEN BEAN-O

Halloween, the gloomiest night of all when the spirits walk and the pooka is abroad, is the perfect night for a BEAN-O party. Invite your guests by phone, or if you prefer write the invitation on a scrap of brown paper.

Come to the BEAN-O party
At Sally's on Halloween night.
It won't be crafty; it won't be arty,
But we'll have fun all right.

Of all the holidays of the year Halloween offers the greatest opportunity for effective decorations. Autumn leaves, cornstalks, and lighted pumpkin Jack-o'-lanterns are traditional and easily prepared. Freehand cuttings (or purchased ones) of witches, pumpkins, cats, bats, elves, fairies, spiders, owls, cauldrons, broomsticks, or peaked hats of black and orange construction paper may be pinned about on the curtains and walls.

Give each guest on his arrival a small cellophane sack containing 150 navy beans. If you can't get the cellophane sacks, a No. 4 or No. 5 brown paper sack will do, but it's more fun to have the transparent sacks. Caution each guest to guard his beans well for with them he'll have to purchase his supper.

As soon as the guests are all assembled tell them that twenty minutes of conversation is in order. During this conversation anyone using one of the pronouns "I," "MY," "ME," or "MINE," must forfeit one bean to the person or persons catching him. There will be some who can scarcely talk without using these vital words while others will get along well. At any rate the exchange of beans will be lively, and the hungry will hoard their beans well because few beans means a small supper.

All teen-agers like popular songs, and most of them are familiar with TV's "Hit Parade" method of dramatizing a song. Suggest that each one take a turn at dramatizing a hit song — without music, of course. For instance, The Rock and Roll Waltz wouldn't be too hard. "One-two, rock; one-two roll." If no one guesses the song being dramatized, the pantomimist receives one bean from each of the other guests. To the correct guesser, the pantomimist pays five beans from his supply.

Circle games are always good. Here is one out of the ordinary. Everyone should sit in a circle on the floor. Tell the guests that each one must name a word beginning with the first three letters of Halloween — Hal, such as Halt, Hale, Halo, Hallo, Half, Halfhitch, Hall, etc. If a contestant can't name such a word before the count of five, he forfeits one bean and the next in the circle takes his turn.

If your crowd likes to dance roll up the rugs and turn on the music. When a boy asks a girl to dance, she pays him a bean. If while dancing he steps on her toe or bumps her into another couple, he pays her a bean. An occasional reminder that a full supper awaits the boy or girl with plenty of beans, adds to the merriment.

In keeping with the Halloween BEAN-O theme, cover the buffet table with brown wrapping-paper, decorated with orange and black cut-outs, or use one of the regular Halloween tablecloths with matching napkins from the dime store. A pumpkin jack-o-lantern lighted by a candle makes a good centerpiece.

Of course, your menu can vary according to your taste but such dishes as Funny face sandwiches, Spook salad, Little Goblin eggs, and Halloween cake are good to eat and fun to look at. Each item on the table should have a card with its name and its cost in beans. As the guests help themselves, a cashier should collect the beans. Some with few beans will look longingly at the un-obtainable items.

After all the guests are seated, and beans collected, a wise hostess will pass "seconds" so that all the guests will have an equal opportunity to share in the food.

Here's hoping you have fun at your BEAN-O party on Halloween.

WHEN SPOOKS PROWL

October brings that bright blue weather poets sing about and it also brings that traditional night of nights when witches, bats, owls, black cats and goblins are on the prowl in step with the moaning wind in ghostly tree tops.

What could be more perfect on such a night than to have the High School gang in for a Halloween party. No other party is such fun to give with all of spookdom ready to do your bidding to add to the party atmosphere. And if you make your party a "superstitious" party you can give your games that different touch that will make your party the talk of the crowd for many a day to come. It will start the social season off with a bang.

Trim your house from top to bottom with black cut-outs of witches riding the broomstick, black cats, owls, and grinning jack-o-lanterns. Add to this usual decoration plenty of superstitious symbols to carry your party theme. Cardboard horseshoes can grace the doorways and huge four-leaf clovers decorate the drapes. In one corner suspend an open black umbrella decorated with bright orange streamers that reach to the floor. This colorful canopy will house your gypsy queen when she tells the fortunes of the willing guests.

Set the pitch for your party with invitations inscribed in white ink on black cut-out skull and cross bones:

BEWARE!

Bring your luck with you
Friday night, October 31
To Bob Wyman's at
8.00 P.M.

YOU'LL NEED IT!

Be a black cat when you greet your guests at the door and hand each one a rabbit's foot to guard him well as he walks under the tall stepladder arching the doorway. Your black-cat costume need be no more than a black-cat mask and a black rope tail fastened under your belt. If the rest of your clothes are dark it will carry the catty illusion.

Usher the girls into a room so dimly lighted they'll not loiter long to primp. A long, jagged, black crayon mark drawn diagonally across the mirror will remind them that bad luck is loose in the house tonight.

A huge number 13 over the door of the boys' room will warn them of the peril of the night as well as huge black-cat cut-outs taped to the walls.

Before the party type a list of Bad Omens or Superstitions, one to a card. Then cut each card into several pieces. Scramble them and place several pieces in each envelope. Hand an envelope to each guest as he enters. By exchanging pieces with the other guests he can get the right pieces to formulate one complete superstition. Here are some familiar superstitions to use:

1. A broken mirror will bring you seven years of bad luck.
2. If you sing before breakfast you will cry before night.
3. If a black cat crosses your path you will have bad luck.
4. To walk under a ladder is extremely bad luck.
5. You'll never finish anything started on Friday.

6. If you put on a garment wrong side out it's bad luck to change.
7. It's bad luck to sneeze before breakfast.
8. It's bad luck to rock an empty chair.

This mixer will give the guests something to do immediately upon arrival and avoid any stilted, awkward moments.

Next seat the guests on the floor in two lines facing each other. Appoint the first man of each line captain. Give each captain a double handful of Bad-Luck Corn. Instruct him to lay his Bad Luck (Corn) in a pile in front of his neighbor. The object of the game is to see which team can first pass the corn down the line and back. Any spilled corn must be gathered up and passed along. It's quite a trick to pass this much corn fast without dropping kernels.

"Bluebeard's Den" is a good chiller-diller. Prepare for it by hanging an old sheet across one end of an adjoining room. Cut four holes in it big enough to admit a head. Just around and below each of these slits smear the sheet with red paint or some kind of red coloring. Catsup will do. Beforehand arrange with one of the fellows to play Bluebeard and ask one of the girls to pose as his first *be-headed* wife. Have powder or flour and a big puff handy so that she may powder her face heavily and quickly. At the appointed time the girl gets behind the sheet, thrusts her head through one of the holes and lets her head hang in a grotesque position.

Dim the lights and call in another girl. As Bluebeard swings his blade or shoots his cap gun accompanied by screams from the two girls, the second girl thrusts her head through a hole in the sheet. Repeat the process with a third and fourth girl. When the heads of the four *be-headed* wives are in place bring the guests, two at a time, from the other room to view the remains. As Bluebeard goes through the motion of showing how he killed each one, the heads moan and scream. This screaming and the report of the cap pistol excites the curiosity of the guests in the adjoining room who are anxiously awaiting their turn to visit Bluebeard's den.

No Halloween party is complete without a fortunetelling stunt. Beforehand have one of the girls prepared to be your gypsy fortuneteller. Under the umbrella canopy mentioned earlier you can make a realistic-looking fire by laying a few sticks across orange tissue paper with flashlights concealed underneath. Burning incense gives the effect of steam issuing forth. Instruct the fortuneteller to question each one about his last dream. She can interpret these dreams according to the following meanings. If you pick a clever gypsy she can also use her imagination and her knowledge of the client to make the fortunes particularly apt. Some common interpretations of dreams are:

> Snakes—deceitful enemies
> Lightning—beware of accidents
> Falling—beware of money losses, hard times
> Crying—joy
> Sunset—love affair
> Fog—end of your troubles is coming
> Writing—will receive an important letter
> Laughing—love or business disappointment
> Suffering—wealth
> Flames—gossip
> Black cat or crows—bad news
> Riding on train—visitors
> Hungry—plenty
> Fighting—success in love, prosperity
> Strange faces—travel

Tell the crowd it's bad luck to follow the leader so you'll play "Contraries." Choose a leader who picks his victim. The victim is to do the opposite of what the leader does. Both are provided with chairs and hats. When the leader stands the victim sits. When the leader puts on his hat the victim takes his off. They should act simultaneously. It is almost impossible to do the opposite while watching the leader, much to the enjoyment of the crowd. After a bit let the victim be the leader and choose some smarty who has laughed long and hard, to be his victim. It's a good game.

Tuna-fish salad tucked into sandwich buns and cheeseburgers are great favorites with teen-agers. Top this off with plenty of cokes or root beer. With some dixie cups and plenty of mints and nuts the refreshment problem is easily solved. Serve these refreshments buffet style and your friends can squat around the fireplace as they eat. Someone will be sure to tell a blood-curdling ghost story.

Try this superstitious party—it's a gang get-together that's really fun.

PUMPKIN IS KING
ON HALLOWEEN

Halloween — What a night for pumpkins! Let's have a party for little pumpkins, fat pumpkins, grinning pumpkins, and snarling pumpkins.

Decorate the house with pumpkin jack-o'-lanterns at your front steps, pumpkin cut-outs pasted on windows and mirrors, paper pumpkins taped to lampshades and pinned on curtains.

Cut your invitations from yellow construction paper in the shape of a pumpkin. On it print with orange pencil or crayons the invitation:

A Pumpkin Party
At Dorothy's
Halloween Day
Three P.M.
Come in costume.

As your guests arrive point to a trail of cardboard pumpkins for them to follow to the bedroom to leave their coats. Then the pumpkin fun begins.

For Pumpkin Golf you'll need a small pumpkin — the littlest you can find. Put the Pumpkin, a bowl and a large spoon on a table. The object is to scoop the pumpkin into the bowl with the fewest number of strokes. Keep score of the number of tries it takes each girl to get the pumpkin into the bowl. To the winning golfer with the least number of strokes goes a pumpkin sticker.

For a Pumpkin Relay divide your guests into two teams, each team forming a line. Give the first player in each line two large orange cardboard pumpkins, about ten inches in diameter. Each player steps on one pumpkin with her left foot and places the other pumpkin as far ahead as she can easily step with her right foot. Standing on her right foot, she picks up the cardboard from under her left foot and advances it ahead of the right foot. The object of the game is to walk across the room and back, stepping on pumpkins all the way. In other words, the player lays her own pumpkin-stepping-stones as she goes. Each member of the winning team receives a pumpkin sticker-medal to add to her array.

To play Pumpkin Hunt one girl must leave the room. Then hide a pumpkin so that the entire crowd except the absent member knows where it is. Call the absent girl back and explain to her that while she hunts the pumpkin the crowd is going to sing "How Green You Are" to the tune of "Auld Lang Syne" — softly when she is far from it, louder as she nears it, and very loud when she gets it. This is a lively game. Each one will want her turn at finding the Pumpkin.

No Halloween party is complete without a fortune-telling stunt so let's try PUMPKINSEED FORTUNES. Give each girl five wet pumpkin seeds. Ask her to stick them on her forehead one at a time. Each one represents a vocation — the first a teacher, second a nurse, third dietician, fourth airplane stewardess, fifth artist. The seeds will stick if pressed tightly to the head. The first seed to drop off indicates the vocation the girl will follow.

Halloween telegrams are always fun for the nimble witted. Give each guest a pencil and paper and ask her to write a telegram using only seven words beginning with the letters of "Pumpkin." For instance, "Please umpire my party. Keen interest now." Allow ten minutes for composition of telegrams. Then collect them and read them aloud. Pumpkin medals go to the author of the message making the most sense, the "corniest," and the most romantic.

When it is time for refreshments cover your table with a paper Halloween tablecloth from the dime store.

Use Halloween paper napkins with a big pumpkin jack-o'-lantern for a center piece. Serve a cup of chicken gumbo soup and nut bread sandwiches, topped off with pumpkin pie for dessert. Make a face on each piece of pumpkin pie with marshmallow for eyes, nose and mouth. Or if you prefer, the features can be made of whipped cream.

By this time all the guests will be ready to take their hard-won pumpkin sticker-medals and go happily home.

MAKE IT A FAMILY AFFAIR

Halloween—that night of nights when all the spooks are on the loose and the witch rides high.

That night our youngsters insist is the proper time for a party—a wonderful party when the *whole* family entertains its friends, children and adults alike. The children avow our family Halloween parties are the best parties of the entire year. And the carefree gaiety of these parties has an equally strong appeal to the adults.

No richer opportunity for effective decoration is given by any season. Autumn leaves, cornstalks, and lighted pumpkin jack-o-lanterns are traditional and easily prepared. Free-hand cutting of witches, cats, bats, fairies, spiders, owls, cauldrons, broomsticks and peaked hats of black and orange construction paper may be pinned about on curtains and walls. And how the whole family loves to help with the cutting.

Candles, dishes of alcohol and salt, and blue Christmas lights make a ghostly illumination. Be sure that all candles are safeguarded to prevent fire hazards.

To convert your lampshades into festive Halloween lights cut strips of orange paper long and wide enough to go around the shade and pin the ends together. Gather the top edge and hold in place with a one-inch band of black crepe paper. Place a black cat or witch here and there on the shade. When the light is on the shades look much more elaborate than they really are.

If your walls are papered you can pin black cut-outs to the wallpaper with common pins. At night the pins do not show and the pin mark is too small to mar the paper. On painted walls stick the cut-outs on with Scotch tape. Witches, bats and cats are very effective when they are Scotch-taped on mirrors and windows.

Black and orange crepe-paper chains are very decorative across doorways or from the corners of the room to the chandelier in the center. Perhaps you remember, from kindergarten days, how to make them. It's easy to do. Take two strips of crepe paper, one black and one orange, of equal length and equal width—two inches is a good width. Fasten the strips together at right angles to each other. Then fold the orange strip over the black, then the black over the orange. Continue until the entire lengths are folded. You will now have a pile of folded squares. Stick or pin the ends of the two strips together. Then pull out the folded papers. You will have a very attractive black and orange chain.

A colorfully decorated home, even though inexpensively done, adds much to the party atmosphere. But the real secret of a successful family party is to have games people of all ages can enter into.

When the big night comes it's fun to have a ghost—junior-size—open the door as the guests arrive and solemnly point to white footprints on the floor. The man-sized (paper) footprints lead to the room where the dads and grand-dads can leave their wraps. The smaller ones lead to the parking place for the women's and children's wraps.

In each of these rooms have large paper sacks to be worn over the head, one for each guest. Before the night of the party cut in each sack holes for eyes, and with black crayon draw on other features, handle-bar mustaches, etc. Also mark on each sack a number to come just below the chin. When wraps are removed, each guest immediately puts on one of the sacks and is given a stiff card and pencil. The object of this mixer is to have each guest list by name and number as many of the paper heads as he can. Of course each person, while trying to discover the identity of others, endeavors to keep himself a mysterious stranger. The one who first completes a correct list of the names of all the guests is dubbed "Chief Paper Head" for the evening.

"Nosey" or "Nose Game" is another good family game which always provides a lot of fun for everybody—parents and children alike. It is a favorite at family parties and you have read a description of it on page 111.

After this teasing game and the well-known, hilarious "Costume Race" relay already recommended on page 113, it is well to give your guests a breathing spell. Ask the youngsters to sit on the floor while you tell them a Halloween story. Assign to each youngster a character which appears in the story. Whenever one's character is mentioned in the story, he makes the sounds assigned to him. The storyteller should pause a moment after a character is mentioned in the story. You'll probably have more guests than characters in the story but two or more can be assigned to the same character. It doesn't lessen the fun a bit.

The "Cat Game" will give your guests a real thrill. It's a must at our family parties on Halloween night. All lights are dimmed. Big and little guests sit on the floor in a circle, a sheet spread in the center. Each one takes hold of the sheet with his left hand and keeps his right hand free under the sheet. The hostess appears holding a tray covered with a napkin and says in a solemn voice:

"This evening when the Halloween cat was on the way to our party it was run over. His remains will now

be passed around under the sheet. This is the cat's eye—
just pass it to your neighbor and so on around the circle
under the sheet." The hostess reaches under the sheet to
hand the first person an icy oyster, to be followed by the
head—a ball of yarn filled with hairpins; tail—a coon tail
from a child's cap; teeth—a string of large beads, chilled;
hide—a brushed wool helmet; tongue—a very cold watermelon pickle; insides—a bunch of soft dough, well
floured. The shrieks accompanying this game are hair
raising.

The refreshments can be as simple or as elaborate as
you want but after an evening of hilarity, apple cider and
pumpkin pie are easy to serve and popular.

By all means give a family Halloween party. It's such a
good chance to have fun with your children and your
neighbors and their children. It also provides a constructive way for young America to celebrate that American
tradition of Halloween merrymaking.

FAMILY FUN AT HALLOWEEN!

Talk about a grand month for parties! No month of the year offers better opportunities for thrilling and original parties than the month of October with its wealth of color and beauty and its Halloween festival.

A Halloween party, which includes the whole family, offers one of the very nicest ways to celebrate this traditional day of merrymaking. Plentiful opportunities for legitimate fun for the young people in the home obviates any desire on their part to participate in activities outside which might easily, in exuberance of spirits, result in depredations and disorders. At the same time civic habits for your sons and daughters are being made.

In our home such a Halloween party for the whole family is an annual event. It has proved so popular with our family and family friends, that each year there is a general request for another. In fact, our sons greatly prefer these family parties at Halloween time to any other kind.

Decorating the house for the Halloween party is one type of interior decoration that boys and girls thoroughly enjoy. All that is needed is plenty of orange and black crepe paper and some black silhouette figures obtainable at the dime store.

At our house "Mike" hangs in the room where the men and boys leave their coats and hats. "Mike" is a life-size cardboard skeleton purchased at the dime store. We painted him over with phosphorous paint (also from the dime store). From the darkest corner of the room "Mike" shines forth in all his ghostly glory, thereby adding to the *spooky* atmosphere of the home.

Guests quickly imbibe the Halloween spirit and are ready for any fun. Games must be planned beforehand and must be for young and old. This is not as hard as it sounds.

A good way to start off the evening is to tell the guests that you have just heard that two witches have come to town and that you suspect they are among the guests; that they must be caught immediately before they can do horrible damage. (Two of the guests have agreed beforehand to be the witches.) The hostess describes the two witches as to height, weight, color of hair and eyes, habits, etc., and adds, if she sees fit, humorous comments. The guests immediately hunt for the two witches that have just been described. As soon as someone believes he has spotted one of the witches he extends his hand and reads in a loud voice from a card (which has previously been given each guest by the hostess) the following:

> When shall we meet again?
> Thunder, lightning or in rain?
> Better take it on the lam,
> Old black witch, beat it, scram!

If he has pointed out the real witch, he or she disappears rapidly through the nearest door. If the discoverer is wrong he gets a Bronx cheer for his efforts. The game ends when both witches have been discovered and sent out.

Another Halloween game which proves a riot, especially for the heavier mamas, is the well-known "Broomstick Game," in which even the men bump their noses and the youngsters rock with laughter watching the grown-ups try this trick of picking up the apple with their teeth. You can read the details on page 112.

The "Pumpkin Carving" contest is always very popular. All the children, big and little, in the party are seated around the room on the floor with papers spread out before them. Each child is furnished with a hollowed-out pumpkin and a knife and told to carve a jack-o-lantern. Mothers and fathers help by suggestions. When the lanterns are finished a lighted candle should be placed in each and the lanterns lined up in a row for decision as to which is entitled to the prize. This is decided by popular applause. Each child may take home his or her own jack-o-lantern.

At our last party, in a secluded corner of the room, was suspended a large iron kettle over a make-believe fire. It had created quite a bit of speculation, but as no one went near it, it was supposedly just a part of the decoration. Just about the time all the guests had forgotten about it, a witch rushed into the room. In a covered basket she had a number of ingredients which were needed for charms. She handed the basket to the hostess and retired to her kettle, muttering.

Each guest was then blindfolded and formed a line. The hostess then explained that all the objects which were in the basket must be passed from guest to guest in the line and finally handed to the witch. It was started off with a hot baked potato which passed quickly from hand to hand amidst sudden exclamations of various kinds. A chestnut burr came next followed by a piece of ice, an old glove filled with mush, a large soup bone, a large peeled grape and an oyster.

The blindfolded guests emitted blood-curdling shrieks as the objects touched their hands. At the end of the line the objects were placed in the kettle and stirred vigorously by the witch while the guests, blindfolds removed, looked into the kettle. When all the ingredients were thoroughly stirred the witch took from the kettle the written fortune of each guest. Halloween is the one night of the year when spirits, according to tradition, roam the earth again and mortals may appeal to them for a glimpse into the future.

At the end of the games big doughnuts were passed on a child's broom handle, accompanied by cider or milk. As an extra treat black-face ice cream was served. This is made by pouring thick chocolate sauce over vanilla ice cream. The eyes, nose and mouth on each serving are marked with tiny mint candies.

Although originally Halloween was a Druid and Roman religious ceremony, in American tradition it is a night of merrymaking, fortunetelling and pranks. Such an opportunity for a good time should not be wasted.

ROLLICKING FUN
FOR HALLOWEEN

Halloween without a party is like bread without butter. It's a season of witchery and fun that demands we humans forget our hum-drum existence for this one night and join the annual frolic of witches, devils, fairies, and other imps of earth and air.

For an evening of rollicking fun invite all your friends and neighbors—young and old alike—it's one party that all can enjoy together.

Turn your imagination loose on decorations. You can be as traditional as you wish, confining your decorations to the usual black cats and bats with black and orange streamers, or you can have very effective decorations with the things at hand.

Shocks of corn stalks banked with pumpkins will change your living room into an outdoor scene. Branches of autumn leaves over the doorways and windows add color. Fat cabbage heads and sturdy turnips make excellent holders for orange and black candles. Shimmering moonlight can be provided by hanging an orange crepe-paper moon in front of a light. With this outdoor atmosphere the tone of your party is set.

A dinner strictly on the Halloween side will start the evening off with a bang. For real fun seat all your guests at one table. Cover it with a Halloween paper tablecloth or plain orange crepe paper. A centerpiece of vegetables with red apple candleholders and orange candles is very effective. Let your fine china along with all the rest of your "best bib and tucker" remain calmly in their accustomed corners while you set your table with shiny tin cups and plates. It's easy to explain that the Halloween witch has made off with all your silver, leaving only the knives.

Serve the food family style direct from the kitchen with no trimmings. A crock of baked beans, escalloped potatoes, and meat loaf served in the tin in which it was baked are substantial mainstays. Make a large flat tin of vegetable salad using orange jello. Cut it in squares in the kitchen and place it on the table as is. Did you ever eat gelatin salad with a knife? Results are most surprising. Escalloped potatoes are not so hard to manage, but the elusive pea—no chance for formality or stiffness. Each diner will be too busy manipulating his knife and laughing uproariously at his neighbor.

Pour the coffee from the big kitchen pot and serve the cream and sugar from the kitchen ware. It will occur to some bright guest to stir his coffee with his knife handle. Soon everyone will be doing it.

Each guest is cautioned to clean his plate thoroughly for dessert. When the plates are cleaned pumpkin pie is passed from the tins in which it is baked.

At the end of this hilarious feast—it will be hilarious I guarantee—you are ready for the games which you have planned so that both Grandpa and Junior can enjoy them.

While you are clearing the table and pushing it out of the way let your guests try this stunt. Hang a string from the center of a doorway. On it fasten a short stick or cane so that it remains parallel to the floor. From one end of the stick suspend a ripe juicy apple. Spin the cane merry-go-round fashion as fast as possible. Then let the first brave soul step close and try to bite the apple as it flies past. If he succeeds in biting the apple he will be, or is, lucky in matters of love. If he fails he's very unlucky and will need considerable dusting off. It's a hilarious game all your guests will be clamoring to play.

For a quieter game give each lady present a cup of wet pumpkin seeds and supply each man, young or old, with a threaded needle. As each lady hands the man a seed from her supply he threads it on a needle and runs it down the thread. If he drops the seed he must recover it before another seed can be threaded. The couple finishing the cup of seeds first wins the right to first try in the next game.

Line up on the table seven lighted candles. Ask a guest to stand six or eight feet from the table facing the candles. Then blindfold him and turn him completely around three times and tell him to walk to the table and blow three times at the candle flames. Allow him three blows and no more. If he blows out all the candles he will sell all his crops at a big profit. If he fails to blow out any he'll have to store his grain. If 1,2,3,4,5, or 6 candles are left burning they indicate the number of years before he will become rich.

This next game can be played by any number of people. Tie candy pumpkins or orange or black jelly beans to a string. Make each string about three feet long. Instruct each guest to put the free end of the string into his mouth and hold his hands behind his back. At a signal all start chewing. They continue to chew until someone gets his piece of candy in his mouth. He is declared winner. It is an exciting game to watch and equally funny to the players who have trouble to keep from laughing as they furiously chew.

While the following game is an old one it always makes a hit. The ladies are seated in chairs facing a circle. There is one extra chair. Behind every chair stands a man. All men stand stiffly with their hands at their sides. The man behind the empty chair is the Halloween cat. When the cat sees a lady he'd like to sit in his chair, he winks at her.

She must slip away from her chair before the man at her back can restrain her by putting his hands on her shoulders. If she escapes her man becomes the cat. If she doesn't, the cat must try another lady. This game is fun for all and takes quite a bit of time. Be careful not to play any game so long that the guests get tired of it. Quit each game while it is at its height and go on to the next game.

For the farewell game let the men join the women in a circle. Caution your guests that no one must laugh during this game. If he does he will be eliminated. The first player, looking solemn, says, "Ho" to the person on his right. That player then says, "Ho Ho" to the third person. He in turn says to the fourth, "Ho Ho Ho." Each person with a straight face adds another "Ho." Around the circle will go the "Ho Hos" until only one "sober-sides" remains. He'll be the winner.

With a merry "Ho Ho" we wish you a jolly Halloween —the night that a party is a must.

THE GOBLINS WILL
GET YOU!

On Halloween, when all the spooks in spookdom are on the loose, it is good to gather close at home and invite your friends in to meet the friendly spooks at your house.

To the children at our house a family Halloween party ranks first. They love to invite their friends and their friends' parents. For us parents there is no grander way to get acquainted with the families of our children's friends. Let us tell you about our last Halloween party.

A week or so before the big night we sent out the invitations in the form of big black cats. The family joined in cutting them out. On the big bushy tails we printed in white ink:

> This is the tail of the Halloween cat,
> Hurry, he says, to meet spook and bat
> On Halloween night, about seven or so
> At a house that you know, yet may not know.
> At 805 Blunt Street— Come in costume and
> BRING YOUR SHIVERS!

Each invitation included every member of the family and was addressed to the entire family.

The front door was fastened with a chain which permitted the spook host to open the door only far enough

to flash a light in the arriving guest's face for the "once
over" before admitting him. Without a word he pointed
to the floor. Two sets of white cardboard footprints led
the way to the several bedrooms where wraps were to be
deposited. The male contingent followed the large footprints; the women and children the smaller ones.

While the guests were gathering much time was spent
in admiring each other's costumes and examining the
house which was decorated for the occasion. All the floor
and table lamps wore Halloween shades. Black and orange
cut-out witches, bats and cats were everywhere on the
walls. Black cats and horrible skulls and crossbones leered
from every mirror. Black and orange crepe-paper chains
were strung across the tops of windows, doorways, and
across the ceiling in the dining room from the center
chandelier to the four corners of the room. With the
dimmed light the effect was weird and highly decorative.

As soon as all the guests arrived each was given a large
spool and one end of a string. These strings had been arranged so that they crossed each other and wound here
and there about the room beneath carpets, around chair
rungs and behind pictures. All led to one large black cardboard spider hanging in the center of the room. At a given
signal everyone began winding. The winner was the one
who reached the spider first with all his string wound on
his spool—he was then given the spider as a prize. Incidentally, this game is a very good "ice breaker." Each
one's undignified scramble for his string removed all
diffidence and everyone was ready for a good time.

A "Cat Race" next kept the guests busy. Before the party
our sons had cut out of black construction paper two large
cardboard cats. A string about twelve feet long was run
through the head of each cat. One end of each string was
tied to a chair across the room high enough from the floor

so that each cat stood on its hind legs. Then the captains of each team took the loose ends of the strings and by jerking them moved the cats down to the man operating the string. The next man in line jerked the cat back up to the chair. Of course, the first line through won the race. It was a hilarious race that left the jerkers helpless with mirth.

The next game was a relay and the guests were divided into two teams. A big orange cardboard pumpkin with a large opening in one side hung in an open doorway. Suspended inside the pumpkin was a small bell. The first man on each team was given a bean bag and told to ring the bell. Each player had one try and then passed the bean bag to the next player. A scorekeeper reported on which team rang the bell the greater number of times.

Then apples were tied to strings in the open doorway. A contestant with hands behind his back tried for a bite at the swinging apple. In a large archway there is room for five or six apples hung side by side. It is loads of fun for the onlookers to watch the struggling contestants.

The "Rainy Day Race" was really hilarious. Once again we divided the guests into two teams. A locked suitcase and an umbrella were given each side. Each suitcase contained rubbers, a skirt, gloves, a raincoat and hat. At the starting signal the leader of each team opened the suitcase, put on the clothing, went out the front door, raised the umbrella and ran around to the back door through the house to the living room, where he closed the umbrella and repacked the suitcase for the next man on his team. Needless to say the repacking and dressing was done at break-neck speed and afforded no end of fun and excitement.

After this riotous event the guests welcomed a chance to catch their breath. While they were resting each one was given a clothespin, a Halloween paper napkin, three straight pins, and a yard of string to make a Halloween table favor.

When the favors were finished and the winners chosen, the guests were led to Goblin's den—our dining room—for the buffet lunch. The tablecloth was black crepe paper. A two-faced lighted pumpkin served the double purpose of centerpiece and illumination. White cut-out skulls and crossbones and large white cat-heads with wide-open mouths and eyes added a lot to the spookiness of the table.

Each guest carried his filled plate to the living room where card tables had been placed. To match the dining table each card table was covered with a black crepe-paper cloth. Scattered over the table top were white cut-out skulls and crossbones. Each table was lighted with an orange candle decorated with a black crepe-paper bow. White grave markers served as place cards. These markers, held erect with stiff cardboard standards, bore such inscriptions as "Here sits spook Tom Jones."

The food too carried out the Halloween idea. Jack-o-lanterns made from red apples were stuffed with tuna-fish salad. Open-faced cheesespread sandwiches with raisin features grinned a welcome. Wedges of pumpkin pie were decorated with skull and crossbones of whipped cream. The children were served glasses of witch's brew (cider) and the adults were given coffee.

After the luncheon all went in to see "Mike"—our family skeleton who holds forth in a dark closet on Halloween night. Mike is a life-size cardboard skeleton purchased from the dime store. We painted his bones with phosphorous paint and he glows realistically from a darkened closet.

By all means give a family Halloween party. It is such a good chance to have fun and be completely natural.

A THANKSGIVING PARTY

Thanksgiving vacation! What a grand time to have a party. Boys and girls love to dress in costume and a nice idea is to ask each guest to come to the party dressed as a Puritan.

A good game to start your party off is "Laughing Handkerchief." Everybody sits in a circle. "IT" holds a handkerchief in the air while everyone laughs. The harder you laugh the more fun it is. Without warning "IT" drops the hanky. When it hits the floor everyone is supposed to stop laughing and immediately put on a "straight face." The last one to stop laughing becomes "IT." This is lots of fun.

When this hilarious game has been played for a bit and while your guests are still seated in a circle, the "Count Your Blessings" game can be played. One child starts off with "I am grateful for apples" or something beginning with the letter "a." The next child is grateful for something beginning with "b" as "I am grateful for my brother." The third "c" might say, "I am grateful for children to play with." So on around the circle and through the alphabet. If a child fails to think of a word beginning with the proper letter he drops out of the circle. The one remaining in the circle longest can be given a chocolate turkey as a prize.

"Indian Trader," an active game, is a nice change after sitting games. Guests divide into two groups and locate at opposite ends of the room. One group is called "Traders" and the other "Indians." The traders decide among themselves upon some vegetable to sell to the Indians. When they have chosen one they march across the room and stand before the Indians. A spokesman says "We have a vegetable to sell. Guess what." As soon as some Indian names the right vegetable all the traders scoot for their own side of the room with the Indians in hot pursuit. If an Indian catches one of the traders, he must join the Indians. Then the Indians take their turn at selling vegetables. This game entertains for some time.

A nice quiet game to follow can be "Questions and Answers," either oral or written. If written, of course, paper and pencils must be furnished. A suitable and not too hard list is:

	Answers
1. What is the Thanksgiving fowl?	Turkey.
2. Who were guests at the first Thanksgiving dinner? . .	Indians.
3. Who were the hosts at the first American Thanksgiving dinner?	Puritans.
4. Name one grain the Pilgrims found in the new world .	Corn.
5. At what time of the year did the Pilgrims hold their first Thanksgiving?	In the Fall after the Harvest.

If desired a small prize may be given to the one answering correctly the most questions.

Nice refreshments are orange ice and gingerbread turkeys. If there is cold turkey in the house turkey sandwiches are good. Then there always is ice cream. Ice cream in turkey molds and cookies in the shape of pumpkins are sure to please your guests.

THANKSGIVING DAY FUN

There's nothing like a bit of fun to chase away that "too full after Thanksgiving dinner feeling." When the grown-ups sit around and talk about Aunt Min's arthritis and Uncle Ed's sick cow, why not add a bit of zip with a few family games?

On Thanksgiving day everyone has had some serious thoughts about the things to be thankful for. Why not suggest it's time for members of the family to pantomime some of their less desirable features for the rest of the crowd to guess? For instance, young George might be thankful for his big feet. He could pantomime how useful they were to him, and let the rest of the crowd guess what it is that he's so thankful for. Still another might be thankful for his muscles, or his brains. Homely Uncle Ted might claim to be thankful for his beauty.

After this bit of horseplay, your crowd might just feel energetic enough for a Cranberry Relay Race. Divide the crowd into two groups. Give the leader of each group four cranberries to put on the back of his hand. He must carry the four cranberries across the room and back and give them to the next in line. If any one of the cranberries drops off, the player must stop and replace it before continuing the race. The line finishing first is the winner.

Another relay that's lots of fun is to give each team leader a pie tin and an apple. At a signal the leader puts the pie tin with the apple in it on his head, runs a set distance, returns, and gives the tin and the apple to the second in line. The first team to finish wins, and the members of the winning team can be awarded candy corn.

A nut-pitching contest is always good indoor fun. For this game put a small bowl in a little larger bowl and place both in the center of a dishpan. Each player then takes a turn trying to throw three nuts into the smallest bowl. Score five points for the nuts landing in the center bowl, three points for the larger bowl, and one point for the dishpan. Let each contestant keep his own score. The player with the highest score gets permission to wash and put away the two bowls and the dishpan.

Perhaps you have some expert whittlers in your family. Even if they are just whittlers try this — give each one a carrot (the short stubby variety are best) and a newspaper to work on. Ask each one to carve a face, figure, or animal — anything he wishes to carve. This calls for creative competition that is often hilarious. A bunch of carrot tops can be awarded the winner.

For an hilarious game try Gobble. Let each one of the group choose the name of an animal. Then ask the most talkative one in the crowd to make a speech about the Thanksgiving dinner. Whenever he raises his right hand, let each one imitate the animal of his choice. When he raises his left hand, everyone remains silent. When he raises both hands, everyone imitates a turkey gobbler. If your speaker is long winded this gets to be lots of fun.

Have a nice Thanksgiving day.

GAMES FOR
THANKSGIVING DAY

In planning programs for children's groups it is well to alternate lively games with quiet ones.

A nice game to play Thanksgiving afternoon is called "Thanksgiving." The players sit in a circle and each one names a word beginning with "T" and ending with "G". The same word cannot be given twice. For instance one may say "Tag," the second "Telling," etc. If player fails to think of a word when his turn comes he drops out of the game. At the end of the game the player remaining is the winner.

It is a good plan to follow a thinking game with an action game. "Electric Shock" is such a game and goes this way: The players line up in two equal rows facing each other. The youngsters in each line join hands. When the whistle blows the first in each line presses the hand of the person next to him; the second person then presses the hand of the third person in line, and so on down the line. As soon as the last player in each line has been reached he holds his hand over his head.

For children familiar with common musical terms the following game is entertaining. Players should be supplied with paper and pencils unless it is played orally. Each sentence or phrase can be completed with a musical term.

Answers

People live in it	Flat
Used in describing a razor	Sharp
Furniture in a store	Counters
Often passed in school	Notes
A person at ease	Natural
Used in fishing	Lines
What one breathes	Air
A part of a sentence	Phrase
Found on a fish	Scales
Another name for a cane . . .	Staff
Shown by a clock	Time
What we should do at night . . .	Rest
Something for a door	Key
A kind of tar	Pitch

A hilarious game is called "Bumpity, bump, bump, bump." The crowd gathers in a circle. The leader gets in the center and starts the game off. She walks up to some person unexpectedly and with her hands at her ears, flapping them like a donkey's, she says very rapidly "Bumpity, bump, bump, bump." The person before whom she stands is supposed to count five before she finishes. If he fails to do so, he takes her place in the center of the circle and she takes his and the game continues. Youngsters think this is good sport.

Siamese singing is always a riot. It will be necessary to have six or seven copies of the words for this song. Give them to one group of the children and ask them to sing the following words to the tune of America:

"O wa ta goo Siam
O wa ta goo Siam
O wa ta goos
O wa ta goo Siam
O wa ta goo Siam
O wa ta goo Siam
O wa ta goos."

It won't take the youngsters long to realize they are sing-ing "Oh what a goose I am." The other youngsters can then sing the following words, also to the tune of America:

> "So say we all of us
> Every last one of us
> So say we all,
> So say we all of us."

I hope you all enjoy your Thanksgiving Day games.

AUNT SUSAN'S
THANKSGIVING PARTY

Family gatherings can be a beastly bore for the children in the group. They get tired and cross thereby making life miserable for the adults and spoiling everyone's good time. It's a wise mother who foresees this and plans entertainment for the entire group; youngsters and oldsters alike.

We all blessed Aunt Susan for her successful efforts along this line when she entertained the entire family last Thanksgiving. Aside from the wonderful eats she planned a glorious good time for the crowd. Even the most boisterous lad was well behaved and had fun.

Upon our arrival at her home she presented each male guest, man and boy, with a wide Puritan collar of white paper, and each maid and matron with a dainty white cap and kerchief made of soft tissue paper. Even nine-year-old Bill with his freckles and missing front tooth looked very angelic in his Puritan attire. Then she pinned on each of us a slip of paper bearing our name for the day. We became Captain Standish, Governor Bradford, John Alden, Priscilla, Humility Cooper, Mistress Katherine Carver, little Peregrine White and the like.

Her dining room was transformed into "Plymouth" by branches of autumn foliage and the green of fir and pine trees. Cornshock tepees with heaps of golden corn and pumpkins served as a reminder that the red man was here on that first Thanksgiving day.

In the midst of this woodsy scene was the Thanksgiving board. A small cabin of Lincoln logs furnished the center piece. Just in front of the cabin a table mirror reflected the miniature evergreen trees and tiny Indian tepees made of brown wrapping paper which bordered the mirror. Tallow candles in pewter holders graced the bare wooden table. Only a minimum of silver was at each place.

Hatchets for the men, guns for the young masters, cradles for the matrons and brooms for the girls, all cut from cardboard, served as place cards.

While the turkey was being carved Uncle John, representing Elder Brewster, read the following, which Aunt Susan had typed out:

"Blessed will it be for us, blessed for this land, for this vast continent. Nay, from generation to generation will the blessings descend. Generations will look back to these scenes of agonizing trial, to this day of small things, and say 'Here was our beginning as a people. These were our forefathers. Through their trials we inherit our blessings. Their faith is our faith, their hope our hope, their God, our God!'"

Aunt Susan's dinner was her usual good feast of roast turkey with dressing, mashed potatoes, squash, cranberry sauce, apple salad, mince pie and coffee.

Back in the living room, after the feast, when we oldsters normally became drowsy and the youngsters fussy or boisterous as their temperaments dictated, Aunt Susan roused us all with a suggestion. She reminded us that as Puritans we still had our houses to build. These forebears of ours were self-sufficient as far as building materials were concerned. They were thrifty too. If one man had more of a commodity than he could use he would trade it for something he lacked. She then gave each of us an envelope of paper money, which was cut from cardboard. Instantly we became merchants, and dealers in house-building materials.

Aunt Susan was the storekeeper. On hand she had a supply of cardboard logs—some twelve inches long, others six inches and still others three inches long. Also a supply of windows and doors cut from cardboard. Each one was given five cardboard logs to start with. The paper cash each had was insufficient to buy a complete house, so it was necessary to barter.

Each of us attempted to build on a flat table or floor the front of a cabin having one window and door. At a given signal the bartering began. It was exciting. Finally Grandpa announced, "My house is done." He received a small saw for his prize.

Next we played "Mayflower." The group was divided into two teams each headed by a captain and formed into two lines. Aunt Susan gave each captain a basket filled with odds and ends—clothespins, pencils, feathers, flat-irons, pillows, nail-files, nails, and matches. The two baskets and contents were exactly the same. The object of the game was to pass all these articles down the line to Plymouth rock and then back again to the Mayflower. The team completing the job first made the losers pay the consequences with an original stunt.

After this excitement we were glad to be seated and play "Dinner." Each person had to name an article of food beginning with a letter found in the word "dinner." The first was "duck," the second "ice cream," etc. The word "dinner" could be used as many times around as desired. Of course, the longer we played the harder the game became because we couldn't repeat any of the foods. When someone failed to think of an article of food he dropped out of the game. Gradually all but Tom was eliminated and he was pronounced winner.

Then someone suggested another dinner game called "Going Out To Dinner." John Jessup and Mary White both knew this game so they started it off. Mary said, "I'm going out to dinner and bring back More Watermelons. What are you bringing back, John?" John said, "I'm going out to dinner and bring back Just Jugs." Then John called on someone else who failed to bring back the right thing. This was continued until the crowd caught on that the articles brought back began with the initials of the first and last names of the person talking.

Aunt Susan's party wound up with a song fest—some old songs for the oldsters and some new songs for the youngsters. All the family felt at the end of the day that this was one family gathering that had been thoroughly enjoyable for all concerned. Aunt Susan had certainly set the pattern for our future family gatherings.

A FAMILY
THANKSGIVING PARTY

Is it your turn to have the family Thanksgiving dinner this year? Of course you love these family Thanksgiving get-togethers but do you get a bit bored to spend most of the day listening to tales of Aunt Jennie's arthritis or your bachelor uncle's gripes about the younger generation? Own up! Naturally you do, and the youngsters get restless and sometimes out-of-hand. Why not avoid all that and surprise the relatives by making a real party of the occasion. It can be done very easily and with only a tiny bit of expense.

Gay autumn leaves made from colored construction paper bearing your invitation will probably surprise your kin if written invitations have not been the family custom. Any little rhyme will serve the purpose as,

> A Thanksgiving party is now being planned,
> For which it is hoped you'll be on hand.
> Don't let bad weather keep you away
> For the clan will gather on Thanksgiving day
> At 805 Blunt Street, 12:30 P.M.

Nothing is more in keeping for decorations at this time of year than colored leaves and harvest fruits. Bright-colored leaves, tips of sumac branches, bitter-sweet berries, corn silks; all gathered at their best and properly pre-served, provide color for the gala occasion. Leaves keep their bright colors and shapes indefinitely if they are dipped in hot melted paraffin and ironed flat. Bunches of corn silks dry straight when hung from the clothes-line and can then be dipped or sprayed in gold paint. Brownish-red sumac can be brightened and preserved by spraying, or if you have no spray, by dipping them in red dye or paint.

For a clever Holiday table centerpiece thrust two nails upright through the center of an ordinary paper plate and then entirely cover with gold paint. Tie the golden corn silks to the nails. Lay the bright red sumac tips around on the plate much like the leaves of a poinsettia.

Arrange green leaves close to the center of the plate and put clusters of bitter-sweet berries on this green back-ground. You will find that you have a most attractive cen-terpiece not only for your Thanksgiving table but for many festive days to come.

It will add to the beauty and color of your table if you arrange colored paraffined leaves on either side of the cen-terpiece to elaborate the pattern to fit your particular table.

The colored leaves also make very pretty place cards. Guests' names can be written on the hard paraffin surface with any opaque water paint. Cardboard standards can be fastened to the backs of the leaves so they will stand upright.

In planning your Thanksgiving feast make it as easy to serve as possible. That usually means serving those foods that can be prepared ahead of time.

To save time and avoid the confusion of serving ap-petizers at the table we like to spread out a serve-yourself arrangement of cranberry cocktail and wafers on the liv-ing-room table. It adds a welcome air as the guests arrive.

Here's a good recipe for cranberry cocktail which, with the exception of lemon and orange juice, can be prepared the previous day. Cook four cups of washed berries in six cups of water until the berries are very soft and mushy. Strain through cheesecloth. Add one cup of sugar to strained juice and heat until sugar is dissolved. Chill. Add the juice of one lemon and one orange just before serving.

For the Thanksgiving dinner roast turkey and dressing, mashed potatoes and gravy, peach pickles, fruit salad, buttered asparagus, hot rolls and jelly are traditional with us. Mince pie and pumpkin pie compete for first place as a favorite dessert with after-dinner coffee.

As soon as the guests are seated at the table and the head of the house is busy with the carving why not give him a break by diverting the attention of the guests while he carves. Have a small pad and pencil at each place. Read the following questionnaire. Be sure to allow enough time for each guest to write the answer to the questions as you read. Here's a sample one that's fun:

1. Name the part of the turkey that assists a lady in dressing .... Comb
2. Name the part of the turkey that opens the front door .... (last part) Key
3. Part of a turkey that appears after Thanksgiving .... Bill
4. Part of a turkey that's part of a sentence .... Claws (clause)
5. Part of a turkey that is used for cleaning .... Wings (dusters)
6. Part of a turkey that the farmer watches carefully .... Crop
7. Part of a turkey that is an oriental .... (first part) Turk
8. Why ought the turkey be ashamed .... **We see the turkey dressing**

9. Why is a fast eater like a turkey? .... Both are fast gobblers
10. What color gets its name from turkey? .... Turkey red
11. When the turkey is cooking what country is he in? .... Grease (Greece)
12. What part of a turkey is a story? .... Tail (tale)
13. What part of a turkey appears on the battlefield? .... Drumstick

By the time the questions are all answered the host will have finished the carving. Collect the answers to be read while the dessert is being served. To the guest with the greatest number of correct answers goes the blue ribbon turkey cut from brown construction paper with a blue ribbon around its neck.

Not too soon after dinner but before that sluggish feeling gets too strong a foothold, why not ask cousin Jim, who usually monopolizes the conversation anyway, to make a Thanksgiving Day speech including in it the names of all barnyard animals. Ask each guest to keep an animal in mind. When Jim raises his right hand everyone immediately imitates the animal he has chosen. When Jim raises his left hand all keep silent. When he raises both hands everyone imitates a turkey's "gobble, gobble." All calls are continued until cousin Jim lowers his arms.

When this talkative cousin declares a truce the family can exercise a bit by trying to pin a head on a turkey. Pin up a picture of a large headless turkey. Then blindfold each guest in turn and give him a try at pinning on the head. The one coming the nearest to hitting the right spot is rewarded with a jar of cranberry jelly.

Here is a game that always creates a riot. Give each guest a slip of paper reminding him that relatives can have good qualities as well as bad. Ask each one to write a trait of character he or she most admires in one of the other guests. To remove all restraint the slips should not be signed by the writer. This always causes a lot of good-natured fun. The slips are then collected and the family virtues read aloud. It's fun to hear just what traits the family most appreciates.

Another game that is a lot of fun is "Family Ties." When the guests are invited ask each male to bring one or two discarded ties. Every man has a few dozen or so which he hangs on to "just in case." Put all the neckties in one basket with the guests seated around the room. The game is to let the rest of the family guess the owner. As each tie is held up for inspection it is greeted with a running fire of comment as to the type of tie it is and what inner urge might make a man buy it. The first person guessing the owner correctly will be awarded the tie.

By this time your crowd should be in a mood for "Family Secrets." Let one member of the group imitate some other member of his particular family in some activity and the crowd guess what it is. For instance, young John may imitate his sister primping for a date. Dad may impersonate mother entertaining the minister at tea. Mother may retaliate by showing Dad trying to borrow a Five from Uncle George.

After these games we'll guarantee all stiffness and boredom will have vanished from your Thanksgiving dinner party. Perhaps you've set the pace for a livelier time at Aunt Jennie's next year, and there is still plenty of time left for a good old-fashioned visit.

A MEXICAN FIESTA

Everyone loves a costume party so why not invite your friends for a Mexican Fiesta with Mexican costumes for your Holiday party. The costumes need not cost a great deal—a wide-brimmed straw hat will do for a sombrero, a bright shawl over one shoulder will serve for a serape for the boys. The girls can wear white blouses with full, bright-colored, ankle-length skirts. On week days the Mexican girls wear rebozos and on Sunday mantillas. The rebozo is a bright-colored scarf worn over the head, and the mantilla is a lace scarf.

"Living Pictures" is a good opener. In this game each guest acts out some Mexican occupation. For instance: One child carries a jar on her head to show how Mexicans carry water; another dances on the brim of a big sombrero to picture their dances; another weaves a bit of rope to represent the making of twine. Playing a guitar, pottery making, etc., all could be acted out. As each one does his stunt the others guess what he represents.

"Sardines," an indoor hide-and-seek game, is fun. One Mexican is "IT" and hides in a roomy place. Then all start quietly hunting for him. As soon as one finds "IT" he hides with him. This goes on until all the children are packed like sardines in one place. It is hard for the hidden ones to keep from laughing as the others hunt.

This lively game can be followed by "Pottery." The

children sit on the floor and with a bit of clay (obtainable at the dime store) model a vase or bowl or any article they want to make. A newspaper may be spread in front of each one to catch falling bits of clay. This is loads of fun and a prize can be given, if desired, for the best modeled article.

A novel way to give your party favors is to follow the Mexican Christmas plan of distributing gifts. Instead of a Christmas tree presents for Mexican children are often put into a clay jar. Christmas eve the children are blindfolded and with a stick they try to break the jar. When the jar is broken the presents fall on the floor and there is a scramble for the gifts. The one who breaks the jar receives a special gift. So why not for your party put your party favors into an inexpensive clay jar and set it on a small table. Let each child in turn be blindfolded and try to break the jar. To him who succeeds in breaking the jar give a special favor.

Novel and easy-to-make refreshments are "Tortillas." They are Mexican corn pancakes. Plain pancakes called Tortillas would do as well. If cake is preferred, one in which a tiny china doll is baked is in keeping with Mexican custom. In Mexico the child getting the doll is supposed to give the next party. A Christmas candle on the cake for each child present, adds to its attractiveness.

GAMES FOR A
CHRISTMAS PARTY

Since the Holiday season is a very special period of the year a party at this time is always more than welcome. The Christmas decorations which are still up save extra work and give the desired festive air.

When entertainment and games have been carefully planned ahead of time the party goes off smoothly without long lapses of nothing to do. The following games have been tried out many times and are most entertaining.

A good way to start off is to hand each guest a pencil and four cards; one card with a band of brown across the top, another blue, another gray, and one of green. Each youngster is asked to list the names of the guests according to the color of their eyes. For instance if Johnny has brown eyes his name goes on the card topped with brown, etc. The youngsters greatly enjoy this game and have a lot of fun discovering the color of their friends' eyes. It's surprising to find how unobserving most of us are.

For a more active game divide your group into two or more teams, depending on the number of players. Line the teams up single file on one side of the room. Set a goal across the room. Mark a starting line. Give the leader of each line two smooth, medium-size buttons. One he places on the starting line, with the other he snaps the first one to the goal as soon as the signal is given. "Snapping" consists of pressing the edge of one button with the other in such a way that the under one flies ahead. As soon as the players reach goal they race back and hand the buttons to the second player in line. The line finishing first wins the relay.

After this rather hilarious game a quieter one called "Shopping" requires that all the children but one sit in a circle on the floor. The remaining one is the "shopper." He stops before one of the seated group and says, "I'm going to Chicago. What can I buy?" He then counts to ten. Before he finishes counting the player before whom he is standing names three objects beginning with the letter "C," as "cats, crossings, or caterpillars." If he fails he must take the place of the shopper. Any city may be named by the shopper, but the articles to be bought must always begin with the first letter of the city named. The children are greatly amused by the weird assortment of objects they are supposed to buy.

Children always like relays. One that can be played in a small space is called "Over and Under." The teams can be lined up as for the button snap game. The first player in each team is handed a bean bag or ball—even a potato will do. When the signal is given he passes this object over his head to the second in line who passes it between his knees to the third who hands it over his head to the fourth. The object goes alternately overhead and between knees to the last one in line who then runs to the head of the line and starts it back over his head. The game proceeds until the line is back in its original order with the first player at its head. The line finishing first, of course, wins the race.

Another active game children enjoy is "Bounce," which can be played with a rubber or tennis ball. Place a waste basket on a chair some distance from the wall. Mark a line about six feet back from the chair on which the player stands. The game is to bounce the ball on the floor so that it goes into the basket. Each one has three trials, as this is not as easy to do as it seems. A point is given for every basket made. After a given length of time points are counted to determine the winner.

After the games and before refreshments the children will enjoy singing Christmas carols, especially the old favorites, "Silent Night, Holy Night," "The First Noel," "O Little Town of Bethlehem" and "O Come All Ye Faithful."

Sandwiches and cocoa are always popular. These can be followed with apples, Christmas candies and nuts.

CELEBRATE THE
TWELFTH-NIGHT

A Twelfth-Night party! What fun! Especially if you borrow a bit from ancient legends and customs to set the atmosphere of the event.

Legend says that all Christmas decorations must be removed by the Twelfth-Night. If left up after January 6th, they will bring ill luck to the house. Legend also says Twelfth-Night ceremonies, properly observed, bring good luck, good health, and prosperity for the whole year. (January 6th is called Twelfth-Night in the northern countries where time was anciently reckoned by nights.)

Invitations may be cut of green construction paper in the shape of holly leaves. Borrowing from the little carol that French children sing, your invitations might read:

> Noel is leaving us, sad it is to tell,
> But he will come again,
> Adieu, Noel,
> Twelfth-Night party
> January sixth, 8 P.M.
> 805 Blunt Street.

Your Christmas decorations are about all the decoration you'll need for this party. However, if you want a dramatic decoration for over the fireplace or on a blank wall, try a large holly bunch. From shiny green oilcloth cut a number of holly leaves. Tape them to the wall. Add three inflated red balloons, and you have a colorful bit of holly — giant size.

Like all successful parties, Twelfth-Night ceremonies take a bit of preparation.

1. By the front door pile a bunch of discarded Christmas greens, cut into small sprigs.
2. Get a supply of good incense that will burn all evening.
3. Make small bundles of twigs or kindling wood (enough to give one to each guest).
4. From your baker buy an over-size loaf of bread, big enough for each guest to break off a piece. Usually this must be specially ordered, although some bakers may know the real Twelfth-Night bread which is used in European countries.
5. From the Library borrow a good horoscope book with outlines of horoscopes for all the months of the year. Lists of lucky stones, colors, flowers, and so on, can be stuck in the book at appropriate places.

You will need your family or several friends to help with the ceremonies. It adds greatly to the atmosphere of the occasion if you and your helpers dress in oriental garb.

As the guests arrive, before they remove their wraps, give a sprig of green to each one with these words: "Speak no word after receiving this bit of Christmas greenery. Proceed in silence to the open hearth, where it must be burned, to destroy ill luck and to make your wishes come true." Direct the guests to an outdoor fireplace or bonfire spot. Caution: Do *not* burn the greens in an indoor fireplace. Greens are most inflammable and might start a dangerous fire.

Have one of your helpers, dressed in red as the Fire Spirit, stationed by the fire, say: "Burn in the flame of this Twelfth-Night fire all bad luck that might visit your house. Make a wish as the greens are burning, and it will come true." After everyone has thrown her greens on the fire, the Fire Spirit continues: "Now you can speak. Proceed to the room of the incense." With that the Fire Spirit points toward the house.

When the guests have removed their wraps show them
to a table on which stands a brazier or lamp containing
smoking incense. Tell the guests: "Inhale this incense
with your nose, your mouth, your eyes and your ears.
Your good health for this year is ensured. Go now and
gather your faggots."

The girl who hands each guest a bundle of twigs
says, "Burn these Twelfth-Night faggots in your own
home, to guarantee a fire on your hearth throughout
the coming year."

Then the guests gather around a table on which the
great loaf of bread awaits. A small piece of the loaf is
broken off by each guest to eat or carry home. The
attendant then says, "This Twelfth-Night bread will
bring plenty to the table of those who eat it and share
it with others."

Following the ceremonies the guests are taken one
by one to the room or corner of the room where the
"astrologer" in gay robes is prepared to read, from the
stars, the future of each one. This does not require
special skill, but the one chosen should be a good
reader. The horoscopes, typed out for each month, can
be concealed in the covers of a large volume, decorated
with signs of the zodiac. They should be expressed in
clear language and can be slightly varied for different
people, even in the same month. The room should be
in semi-darkness, though the "seer" will need a reading
light.

After all this ceremony, the girls will be glad to try
their ingenuity in design. Seat your guests around a table
and place in the center a big bowl of styrofoam balls of
various sizes, ranging from the big three-inch balls, to the
little half-inch balls. Also furnish a quantity of pipe
stem cleaners and a dish of sequins, and a paper of
pins. The only tools needed will be an ice pick and some
scissors.

Offer the girls a prize for the best snowman. It might
be wise to have one made as a sample. Using the big
three inch ball for the body, push the ice pick through

the upper part so that you can force a pipe stem cleaner through for arms.

For the head join the two-inch ball to the body with a pipe stem cleaner. With pins stick on sequins for eyes, nose and mouth.

Insert pipe stem cleaners in the body for legs. Thread two half-inch balls onto each cleaner to make chubby legs.

A simpler snow man can be made with three balls — the largest for the bottom, the second size for the body, and a small one for the head. These are all joined by pipe stem cleaners.

The girls will have fun making clownish looking snowmen and will love the competition.

By this time, everyone will welcome refreshments. Your Twelfth-Night table can be as elaborate or as simple as you like, but it must be attractive. For an easy practical tablecloth use a piece of nylon net large enough to cover your table. Decorate the net around the edges with clusters of holly leaves cut from green felt, and round red felt holly berries.

Use this net cloth over your regular tablecloth. In the center of the table arrange the large-size holly decoration described earlier — the green oilcloth leaves and three red balloons. Add red candles at each end of the center piece, and your table will be lovely. The nylon net cloth can be saved until next season, and your regular tablecloth will be unharmed.

Cakes have always been associated with the Twelfth-Night feast. As late as the nineteenth century, every French, Dutch, German and English family had its Twelfth-cake. The Twelfth-cake is a dark cake, rich with fruit and spices, heavily iced and decorated with gold and silver stars, many colored flowers and little figures of Three Kings. The cake always contains a bean and a pea.

For your refreshments why not have a bean and pea inserted into a fruit cake and decorate it appropriately.

The girl who finds a pea in her portion becomes Twelfth-Night Queen, and the girl who gets the bean is her Lady-in-Waiting.

For a beverage serve a soft drink of your choice.

Each departing guest takes home as a souvenir of this Twelfth-Night party, the snowman she created and her bundle of faggots to burn for good luck.

Everyday Fun with Youngsters

FUN FOR
LITTLE LONESOME

Have you a little "Lonesome" at your house, who has no playmates near his age and is too young to fare "abroad"? If so, you're well acquainted with the wail, "What shall I do now, Mother?" or "There's nothing to do." Wishing he were a twin, or old enough to read, will get you nowhere. Far better to be ready with a suggestion or two for fun.

A delightful, entertaining toy for small children is a flying bird. Cut the little six-inch body from cardboard. Let "Little Lonesome" color the body with crayon and paint a bright eye on both sides of the body. Then cut a slit for wings through the body near the shoulders. A slit at the rear will allow the tail to be slipped into place and glued into position.

The colored wings can be made of colored construction paper or even tinted stationery, and folded in bellows fashion, back and forth, in one-inch folds. Slip wings through wing slot. Cut the tail from the same kind of paper in V-shape, and fold in one-fourth inch folds toward the point of the V. Glue the tail in position. Punch a hole in the back of the bird for a string. Attach a bird to the chandelier or in an open window or on the porch. "Little Lonesome" will adore watching him fly. A four-year-old will quickly catch the trick of making the birds and soon have a family of flying friends.

An elf garden will bring endless delight to any youngster. Get him a flat box, such as is used in greenhouses to start plants. Line the box with heavy tar paper to keep the wet earth from soaking through. Put in a layer of rich earth. Let him place a small mirror — one from and old purse will do nicely — for a lake. Then suggest he lay out a garden. Evergreen twigs make excellent trees, and slips from colored foliage plants make colorful borders. Grass, planted in the open areas, if well watered, will sprout in three days. A sand walk with pebble borders will add to the view. Such a garden will delight any child, and its possibilities for development are endless.

For the runabout who likes activity try a homemade hobby horse. An old sock stuffed with newspapers and mounted on a broomstick is quite satisfactory. Crepe paper, strips of old cloth, or yarn can make ears and a tail. Black oilcloth strips make wonderful halter and reins. With such a horse "Gene Autry" will ride again and again.

Don't overlook the card table house that calls for only a blanket thrown over a card table. Such a shelter can be a house for a while, with a full scale tea party in swing, then quickly change to a zoo for wild animals with animal crackers in paper cages. Cut strips of paper to make the partitions for the cages. Or it can be a school house with teacher talking to imaginary pupils. Just a suggestion or two from mother will bring magic into play.

Another project is that of rock paperweights. If Johnny can find or has collected some nicely shaped rocks, let him clean them thoroughly and then paint them for gay colored paperweights. Collecting stones with a purpose will fascinate him. Perhaps he can make some rock paperweights as Christmas gifts for his aunts and uncles. This added incentive will give him zest for his work.

For pure fun please don't overlook the indoor sandbox. It sounds gruesome, but a box of clean white sand in the basement will provide hours of entertainment for any youngster. The fine white sand tracks very little, and the extra work it makes will be more than offset by the fun it provides for the child.

A busy child is a happy child, and chances are, that the youngster who learns to play alone contentedly will never develop whining habits that will make him unpopular when he reaches the company stage.

MAGIC BOX

On the very top shelf of her closet Mother kept a Magic Box for fun on rainy days. No sudden spring shower, no summer downpour was sufficient reason for producing the Magic Box. But when we awakened to the drip, drip, on the roof and saw the lowering clouds that would keep us housebound we thrilled with expectancy. On such a day Mother would bring out the Magic Box.

Mother's Magic Box was filled with suggestions for play. She would hold the Box just above our heads. We'd stand on tiptoe, reach in and draw out a slip. Mother would read the slip which decided our pastime for the next hour or so.

If the slip said Muffin Pan Polo we'd get out Mother's muffin tin and six of our little wooden inch-square blocks. Standing about five feet away we tried to toss the blocks into the muffin tin compartments. For every cube that stayed in the pan we won some raisins. Excitement ran high and we always overplayed the allotted time.

If the next slip read "Bicycling" we knew what to expect. We'd lie on our backs, lift our feet and pretend to ride a bicycle. Mother busy at the table would call out "slow; now fast; here's a hill; coast, turn to the right to pass this car coming; stop, you're home now." We never played this too long, but I know now it used up a lot of energy.

Children are always responsive to the imaginative touch. A ball easily becomes a fox or a rabbit. A handkerchief can become a snake with the greatest of ease. Nursery rhymes came for their turn. At a suggestion from the Magic Box we became "Jack-be-nimble" or "Little Miss Muffet." We dearly loved acting out these and other Mother Goose characters.

The Magic Box version of playing horse included a chant, all of us impersonating the pony. The chant goes like this.

> Trot, trot, trot, little pony, trot
> Down the road so rough and stony,
> Trot along my little pony.
> Trot, trot, trot, trot, trot, little pony, trot.
>
> Run, run, run, little pony, run!
> Run along and do not stumble,
> Or I fear we both shall tumble.
> Run, run, run, run, run, little pony, run!
>
> Rest, rest, rest, you have done your best.
> To the stable I will lead you
> And on hay and oats I'll feed you,
> Rest, rest, rest, rest, rest, little pony, rest!

While the first verse was being chanted, we'd raise our knees very high without moving forward. We'd run during the second verse and be fed and put into the stall during the last verse.

These were some of the fun suggestions kept in Mother's Magic Box for Rainy-day pleasure while we were housebound. Mother's Magic Box not only supplied us with fun while we were kids, but left us with pleasant memories of the so-called dismal, dreary days.

STARCH AWAY
RAINY DAY BLUES

A little rain must fall in everyone's life, we are told, but when it pelts down day after day making prisoners of your small fry, they are sure to rebel. They get bored with their playthings, whine for something to do, and fight with each other. However, before you reach the screaming point, you can turn this "drizzling day" into one long to be remembered as "Starch fun day."

Everyone has starch of some sort in the house, either dry or liquid. The children can turn into artists or sculptors. With starch youngsters can finger paint, make flowers, decorations for Halloween or the Fourth of July, model puppet heads, build log cabins, make spangly costume jewelry, create fascinating animals, and make Christmas ornaments. The possibilities are limited only by the artists's imagination.

If you have liquid starch in the house you are all set. If you happen to have dry starch, here's a recipe used by a kindergarten teacher for her class fun.

Dissolve one-eighth cup of laundry starch in a half cup of cold water. Slowly add to a pint of boiling water and cook about five minutes, stirring constantly to keep the mixture smooth.

For finger painting, whether you are using the commercial liquid starch or some you have just made, divide it into three different containers. Color each portion with a few drops of vegetable coloring for a different shade.

Most youngsters get acquainted with finger painting in school, but if yours haven't reached the school age the instructions are simple. Any large sheet of white paper — wrapping paper, shelf paper, or even typing paper will do for a start. Wet the paper on both sides with a sponge or cloth. Better mark the dull side of the paper with an "X" to distinguish it from the shiny or work side.

When children are covered with protective aprons, they are ready to go. They can paint with their fingers, palms, or heel of the hand. Anything goes and each method gives a different effect. Finger painting will dry in an hour or so, but to prevent curling thumbtack it to a molding board.

As your youngsters get more adept in creating unusual finger painting designs they may want to decorate greeting cards or note paper. These can be made on plain or heavy note paper in any desired size. Suggest the kids decorate some note paper for their own Christmas "Thank you" notes. That'll add zest to the project.

Another idea: Finger painting can be taped with transparent tape around a waste basket with effective results.

Perhaps the youngsters will enjoy making flowers. Let them finger paint tulips, roses, daffodils, pansies or any of the simpler flowers. On separate sheets of paper, finger paint blossoms and leaves. Allow to dry. Cut them out and staple or paste them together.

An attractive container for flowers can be made with finger painted swirls, also neatly pasted or stapled together.

Starch sculpture is fascinating and also painless, because there will be no nicked fingers in the process.

With the uncolored liquid starch — either bought or made — and facial tissues or sawdust you can get perfectly hard paintable surfaces. When still wet these materials are easily modeled. With this combination you can create puppet heads, table centerpieces or figurines — take your choice.

Children usually like to make puppet heads. For a head you need a cardboard tube large enough for a finger to enter — newspaper, facial tissue, string, rope, yarn, beads or buttons.

Crumple newspaper into an egg shape about three inches in diameter. Stick ends of newspaper into three inch cardboard tube which forms neck of puppet. Fasten to tube with string.

Soak several facial tissues in liquid starch and model on egg-shape foundation. (Very soft toilet paper will do as well.) Make nose and features of puppet by building up layers of wet paper. Allow to dry. Cover the rest of the egg-shape with three-inch squares of tissues soaked in starch. Then give the entire head surface a final coating of starch-dipped paper to insure a smooth hard finish.

When dry, paint entire head with flesh toned paint. Allow to dry once more. Mix water colors with starch and paint in desired features.

Frayed rope fastened with glue can be used for hair. Beads, thumbtacks or buttons can be eyes.

Perhaps your youngster will enjoy making animals. If so, let him roll up a newspaper to form the basic parts of his animal. These parts are tied together in the general shape of a polar bear, giraffe, horse, or whatever he imagines his animal to be. Next the form is covered and filled in with strips of newspaper dipped in or covered with uncolored liquid starch.

This is allowed to harden. Then the animal is ready to be painted imaginatively or realistically with water colors. A coat of shellac may be added to preserve the work.

Another delightful project is starch modeling which calls for starch and sawdust. Use $1\frac{1}{3}$ cups of sawdust to each cup of liquid starch — or until the mixture feels right for modeling. This mixture can be put on any base, such as a cardboard box house.

Cut and shape a cabin from a cardboard box. Put on the starch mixture and let dry. Groove the mixture to represent logs. The result will be a natural wood-color log cabin, which the youngsters can paint if they wish.

Little girls will love to make starch jewelry out of string and pins. Cut and tie string in any arrangement you desire such as a star, a cross, a circle, or just a group of loops. Lay it on a flat surface and secure it with straight pins. Coat finished design liberally with any color starch and allow to dry. Remove pins and glue a safety pin on back side. Little Susie will proudly wear her ornament on her coat or dress.

The decoration possibilities of starch creativeness are endless. For instance, delightful Christmas tree ornaments can be created by small fry. Bells and Yuletide designs can be finger painted and stuck to string, or designs can be made of stovepipe wire and covered with starched tissue paper.

At Easter time a stained glass window is fun. Color your starch with various Easter egg dyes. (Dilute the Easter egg dyes in a teaspoon of warm water and mix with liquid starch.) Let the youngster stain the window to suit his taste. Give a leaded effect to the window by placing small strips of black paper on the pane while still wet.

On the Fourth of July, the flag can be painted on the window. To achieve real white stripes mix one part cleansing powder to two parts of liquid starch.

On Halloween the possibilities are endless for painting witches, black cats, and broomsticks on the window. And Mother, you won't have to worry because starch designs are easily washed off.

Perhaps you can think of other delightful ways to turn a dismal rainy day into creative fun.

FUN IN YOUR
OWN BACKYARD!

Just outside our back door is a vacation spot that our youngsters claim is tops for sheer fun. It is our own backyard recreation center that we created to solve the problem of idle vacation hours for our active sons and their friends. In the past our boys, like the others in the neighborhood, always greeted the summer vacation with unrestrained joy, but soon came the complaint heard all too often, "What can we do now, Mother?" We no longer hear this since we made our home playground.

Our backyard is typical of the ordinary city backyard; forty by fifty feet. Gone are the once gorgeous perennials, the rock garden and the beautiful fish pool. In their places are a number of attractions that delight the heart of any boy, and incidentally keep him very busy. We decided to devote one side of the yard to permanent play equipment, while we kept the other side free for games.

First we discovered that such a playground must be enclosed to keep all activities within our own yard—an arrangement any neighbor appreciates. Fences are expensive, and we wanted our budget to provide as much play equipment as possible. After giving the matter some thought we decided upon a four-foot-high snow fence. It's inexpensive, easily erected, and is not unsightly. It comes stained red but can be easily whitewashed or painted. It not only keeps the youngsters in but also acts as a backstop for balls.

When the fence was properly in place we had to choose equipment. By popular vote a "gym" was first. There are various types available on the market. The type with double apparatus repays you in satisfaction. There is something in children that makes them want the swing or trapeze at the same moment someone else does; hence the advantage of the twin feature.

A source of lasting pleasure to youngsters is our teeter totter. This was easily made with a sawhorse and a heavy plank. Cleats nailed across the underside of the plank near the center prevent it from slipping.

The sandbox is a tradition in American childhood. A plain box filled with sand can be glorified by the addition of four legs, benches attached along the sides, and a top of boards or canvas. The benches not only afford comfortable positions for the children while playing in the sand but do away with the problem of sand being carried into the house on small shoes—a fact appreciated by busy mothers.

In the far corner of the yard we have built a brick fireplace. This fireplace can be as simple or as elaborate as one wishes. Ours is a small one, sturdily built, using only three dozen bricks, but it draws well. It never loses interest for the youngsters, to say nothing of the oldsters. The boys love to do outdoor cooking. Wieners and buns, potatoes and husk-wrapped ears of sweet corn baked in hot coals, and dessert of toasted marshmallows is a favorite. The boys are very proud when their parents are guests at such a meal.

Perhaps you are thinking that the mosquitoes are also guests at such a meal. That problem was solved for us by building a screen house, also a family project. We had no blueprints. Its size was regulated to our needs. It was high enough to admit without stooping our six-foot Daddy. We covered the frame, which was made of crating lumber, with fine wire screen and purchased a ready-made screen door. The roof is of heavy, water-proof awning cloth. A picnic table and benches for five people makes for comfort, not only for eating but for handwork and games.

During the winter months we slide the screenhouse into the unused side of our garage. If the sides of the screenhouse are made of screen windows hinged together, it can be folded during the winter months.

The side of the yard reserved for such games as croquet, juvenile badminton, and quoits, is bordered on the west by the garage. So that these games might be played after dark as well as in the daytime we hired an electrician to install an outdoor floodlight. Such lighting is not expensive and permits enjoyment of games during the evening. It also means no game must be left unfinished because of darkness.

Hitting the bull's-eye in a game of archery is much more intriguing and safer than shooting arrows wildly about in closely populated neighborhoods. So we set up an archery target using the garage for a backboard. The target is painted on wallboard which is backed by a thick layer of straw.

A basketball basket is also fastened to the garage wall. Youngsters love to shoot baskets and have devised various competitive basketball games.

For everyone's convenience we have one hard and fast rule. All game equipment must be put into a place provided for it when the game is finished. Shelves that provide such a place were put in by the boys and their Dad inside the garage along the far end just high enough to miss the nose of the car when it is parked in the garage.

On these shelves are kept basketballs, horseshoes, shuttlecocks, rackets, and whatever other equipment is needed for the games. The boys soon learned that it is well worth their time to return each piece of equipment to its proper place on the shelves. It's such a nuisance to be continually hunting some piece of equipment whenever you want to start playing. Incidentally, the lesson of order is instilled without tiresome lectures.

For wintertime fun we convert that portion of our yard kept free for games into a skating rink. A skating rink is quite easily made with some snow, some water, and a little work.

First we make a wall around the rink of snow scraped from the area. The wall need only be ten or twelve inches high. Then we freeze the wall by sprinkling it with a garden hose which we connect to the laundry faucet in the basement and run through the basement window. At this time we also sprinkle the scraped ground to give a base for future applications of water.

After the wall and ground are coated with ice we add enough water to cover the whole area. This first water will fill the small depressions in the yard. After these are filled and frozen over, enough water is added to make a smooth surface. The rink comes out smoother if a small quantity of water is added at a time. It will take two or three applications before the rink is smooth enough to skate on. When the ice becomes roughened by too many skaters another coating of water will restore its smoothness.

Some springs we have found that the grass is not as thick where the rink was as it should be, although the grass has never died out entirely. We have discovered, however, that any bare spots caused by the ice or left by moving any of the play equipment can be readily repaired by the sowing of a generous amount of rye seed mixed with the grass seed. The rye comes up in two or three days, protects the slower grass growth, and can be mowed with the lawn mower.

Too much cannot be said in favor of a backyard playground. Your youngsters will be happy and busy having a good time and will be sharing their activities with all their friends. Also—and this is important—when the youngsters are in your own backyard you can unobtrusively keep an eye on them and know they are safe.

TALK GAMES FOR
FAMILY FUN

We play Patty-cake with our babies, Ride-a-cock-horse with our toddlers, and Peek-a-boo with the little ones—then most of us stop playing games with our offspring until they are mature enough to challenge us to a game of bridge.

And that's our big mistake. We shouldn't miss a single chance for fun with our children because we don't have too long a time together. Oh, I know when Jim comes in with a black eye or bloody nose day after day you wonder, "Will he ever grow beyond this fighting stage?" But this troublesome noisy period between cuddly babyhood and interesting young adulthood only lasts about nine years—the grade school years. And if we don't enjoy these young pugilists and tumble tomgirls right now we are losing a wonderful chance to establish pleasant relationships with them that stand us in good stead when they reach the supposedly difficult teens.

One time when we were talking about family games, one hardworking mother, hands on hips, snorted, "Humph! With all I have to do I should play games, yet!" She didn't realize that it doesn't take extra time to enjoy a few family games. These games really only take the time often used by brothers and sisters for bickering, or by parents with scolding and worrying.

For instance, at our house when the youngsters during lunch begin to argue, and whose don't, it's fun to say, "I'm going to Chicago. What shall I buy?" Immediately the game is on. The child to my right will respond with three things beginning with the first letter of the town I mentioned. In this case he might answer, "Cows, cats, and corn." Then he says that he is going to St. Paul and his brother must name three purchases beginning with "S." The rules of this game say that these three items must be mentioned before the next player can count to ten, but for a game to be played during lunch or dinner, we eliminate the excitement of the speed tests and play the game without it. It provides much merriment and takes no more talking than more unpleasant subjects.

Another good game to be played during mealtime we call "Cities." Dad says, "I'm going to Austin." The next one at the table names a city beginning with the last letter of the town mentioned. In this case he could say "New York." That makes the next one search for a "K" like Keokuk or Kalamazoo or Kansas City.

"Cities" has always been a special favorite with our family. We've played it not only during lunch, but in the car when the children get restless, or while we're cleaning up the living room. You'd be surprised how much more willing boys and girls are to dust or wipe the dishes when there's a game on.

"Snap" is a jolly game that in-betweeners enjoy. Start the game off by pointing to one of the family circle, pronounce a word, then spell it, such as "Dog. D O G." Then immediately count to twelve—then say "Snap." Before you reach twelve the lad or lass to whom you have pointed must name three objects, the first beginning with D, the second with O, and the third with G. If he doesn't finish before you say "Snap," he is "IT" for next time. Words of more than three letters can be used after a little practice in the game.

Because there's a bit of actor in each of us, most everyone enjoys "Adverbs." Mother thinks of an adverb and then proceeds to do what the players request her to do in the manner of the adverb she has thought of, such as "Wearily," "Hastily," "Ardently," etc. Then the group tries to guess what the adverb is.

Another talk game that can be played anywhere or anytime is "Proverbs." This is enjoyed by youngsters a bit older. One thinks of a proverb. The others ask any questions they please, but in his answer the thinker-upper must use one word of the proverb. The questioner tries to discover the significant word in each answer until he can guess the proverb chosen. For instance, perhaps the proverb chosen is, "All that glitters is not gold." The questioner might ask, "Is your dress new?" and the answer might be, "Yes, but it doesn't glitter."

The person who first guesses the proverb thinks up the next one.

With the dinner work cleared up happily and quickly sometimes there is time left for table games before study or bedtime. When I was a youngster I thought of chess as an old man's game, but today's youngsters enjoy chess from the time they are about eight.

But if you don't care for such a time-consuming game, there are many other familiar games that you should haul out and brush off for fun with the youngsters. Such as checkers, tiddlywinks, parchesi, and all sorts of card games. And if you have an idea that canasta is only for the grownups just try the youngsters. They love it and will give you a race to win.

Incidentally there is no place like game time to teach the small fry good sportsmanship. Unless of course in your family Dad always has to win. One young lad once told us, "At home we have to let Dad win every game."

That Dad was only a spoiled boy grown tall. But we can use family game time to teach our own youngsters to take defeat gracefully, to win without too much gloating over the loser, and to accept parents as people and not as consciences on legs that catch them when they are doing wrong.

The youngsters won't be the only ones who will benefit from family games. Before you know it, you'll be looking forward to those rainy vacation days when Jack and Jill must stay in the house. Fun and laughter will replace the restless scrapping and bickering that now make those days unpleasant.

THE BASEMENT
CAN TAKE IT!

Have you thought of your basement as an activities room for your youngsters? We are not thinking now of an expensive amusement room nor a colorful rumpus room, but just plain basement. We are so used to thinking of the basement in terms of laundry and furnace that many of us have never even thought of it as a big, uncluttered place for youngsters to play on the days when for various reasons they can't go outside.

For the little tousled-heads that are always under foot on rainy or sub-zero days a sandbox of white sand in the pleasantest corner of the basement provides endless entertainment. The youngsters soon learn to keep the sand in its box and there is no more likelihood of sand being tracked upstairs than there is of its being tracked into the house from an outdoor sandbox.

All small fry love to swing. Rope swings swung low can be fastened to the heavy crossbeams of the basement ceiling.

Children a bit older get a lot of fun from bean bags. A clever bean-bag board can be made from a board about two feet wide and two and one-half or three feet long. Holes must be cut in it for eyes, nose, and mouth. The openings for the eyes should be about seven inches long and five inches wide. The mouth should be about four inches long and ten inches wide. The base of the nose triangle should be about eight inches long. This board can be placed either against the wall or supported by a hinged prop.

If the children want to make a regular game of it and keep score, they stand in line ten to fifteen feet from the board. Each player has five bean bags, or five bags may be used by several players playing in turn. A bag thrown into the mouth counts five points, one into the nose ten points, and for each eye twenty points. The first player to get one hundred points is declared winner.

The basement floor makes an ideal roller skating rink. While the younger ones are perfectly happy skating the older ones crave a little more excitement and the smooth basement floor becomes a rink for "Rollerskate Polo." This game is a product of our boys' imagination, is fast and furious and is a vent for excess steam. Each player wields a croquet mallet but only one ball is used. A goal is set up at each end of the basement and the game is on. The boys choose sides and each team tries to get the ball into the opponent's goal. The team first making five goals is the winner.

Another original roller skating game is an "Obstacle Course." Tin cans salvaged from the rubbish box are set up at various distances and skaters maneuver through the openings between cans much as a skier maneuvers around trees on an open hillside.

Tin cans and croquet balls are all the equipment needed for an indoor "Bowling Game." Ten tin cans are set up in ten-pin formation. One point is given for every tenpin knocked over and fifteen is scored if all the cans fall at one shot.

Less noisy but still lots of fun is a "Jar Ring Toss." A board about twenty-eight inches square is prepared by driving at an angle twenty-three nails three inches long part way into it or by screwing into it little right-angle hooks like those used to hold curtain rods. Each hook is given a value of twenty-five, twenty, fifteen, ten or five points. Figures can be cut from a calendar and pasted on.

The board can be hung against the wall or set on a table. Its center should be about shoulder high. The players stand ten feet from the board. Each is given twelve rubber jar rings, which he tries to throw onto the nails or hooks having the highest numbers. The players throw three times in a play and rotate four times. It is well to mark the rings with crayon or paint so that each person may identify his own in counting the final score.

"Miss the Bell" is a game that's fun and easy to arrange for. A bell is suspended in a hoop about eight inches in diameter and a small ball is given to the players. They take turns tossing the ball through the hoop without causing the bell to ring. One point is scored each time the ball goes through and three points are scored if the bell does not ring.

"Basement Button Snap" is our glorified version of tiddlywinks. Draw two chalk lanes about a foot wide along the floor and supply each player with two buttons. One he places on the staring line. With the other he snaps the first one down his lane to the goal as soon as the signal is given. Snapping consists of pressing the edge of one button with the other in such a way that the under one flies ahead. If a button leaves its lane it must be put back at the starting line and snapped on its way again. Obstacles over which the buttons are snapped add interest to the game. The player who first drives his button to the goal wins the game.

"Barrel Toss" is a good game for a change. The players stand about twenty feet away from a barrel and throw stones or wooden blocks into it. Each may have five throws and a point may be awarded for each stone or block that goes in. The throwing line may be put farther back when the players are experts.

Boys always like to wrestle and tumble and practice rolls and falls. These lads will have endless fun if you put an old mattress on the basement floor. The boys will need no rules or encouragement to start their fun. They'll soon create their own contests and maybe get Dad to join the fun.

For children old enough to play with sharp-pointed darts, here's a homemade game that's fun. Make three darts by cutting the heads from matches. Slit one end so that a piece of folded paper about two and one-half inches square can be slipped into the slit. Into the other end of the match force the eye-end of a large sewing needle. A circular target whose outside circle is not more than fifteen inches in diameter is drawn on a wall board or a piece of heavy cardboard and hung shoulder high on the wall.

The players stand about eight feet away from the target and each tries to throw the three darts so as to pierce the target as near the bull's-eye as possible. For each dart that sticks firmly in a space the player receives the number of points marked in that space. Nothing is counted for darts touching a line.

Turn your youngsters loose downstairs where the walls won't mar and the floors won't scuff. The kids will have fun and you'll enjoy the quiet order of your living rooms.

TAKE THE YOUNGSTERS
WITH YOU

We have made many trips by car from Minnesota to Florida, and from Minnesota to Texas, not to mention numerous shorter trips—with two small active boys as passengers. If we have learned nothing else we have learned this, that if both you and the children are going to enjoy your vacation by car you must plan for it.

You can't take an active youngster, plop him down in the car with nothing to do except to ride all day, and have the youngster happy. Or if he is, I'll guarantee *you* won't be, because if small youngsters don't have something definite to do, they'll find something to do, and it may not be in accord with your idea of the proper occupation for a passenger in your car.

We acquired our boys one at a time so when we made our first trips, we had just one small son to cope with. One of the first things we learned was that the youngster wanted to see what was going on. A most natural desire. Can you imagine yourself riding all day and only being able to see bits of the sky as you look up at an angle through the car window? A child's auto seat is a great convenience, but in many instances we found it took too much space. As a substitute we purchased a small straight red chair. The child loved the color. We placed it in the seat between Daddy and Mother. This enabled our young lad to see out the front or side windows with the greatest of ease. From this seat he would ride contentedly for long periods. When he became sleepy it was easy to shift him to our laps or lay him on the back seat for a snooze.

But time went on and we acquired another boy. We still loved to travel. But two small, active boys are more than twice the problem of one. When two boys have nothing to do they can always wrestle, which is bad for luggage and for parents' morale. Then too they can fight, which not only upsets the adults but the children as well. So we learned to plan.

In the first place we try to make as much use of the car trunk for luggage as possible, to allow plenty of room in the back seat for the youngsters. We try to use judgment in deciding on what we can get along without.

Before starting on our journey we have found it wise to talk over the trip with the lads. We show them on the map just where we plan to go, and about how long we expect to be en route, and what there'll be to see along the way. You'll be surprised how it helps if your youngsters know ahead of starting time that they will be riding all day for several days in succession.

We plan with the boys what toys they would like to take along to play with in the car, restricting each to a small bag container. We have found such things as small mosaic blocks, small cars and airplanes, color crayons, books to color, and packages of colored construction paper ideal to take along. Such things require little space and provide much entertainment.

Endless snowflake designs can be made from toilet tissue by tearing off the little squares and folding them into smaller squares, and clipping off various corners with round-tipped shears or making notches in the sides or centers. When the squares are unfolded each one is different and surprisingly attractive. To add to the fun the flakes can be colored, even though we've never seen purple snow.

In addition to the things the boys take with them we have a surprise box. From the dime store we buy small articles and wrap them in separate packages to be opened on the way. On one of our last trips we purchased a small cardboard barn of the folding variety, which was set up on the ledge above the back seat in the car. This was surprise package Number One. Packages for the following days were small animals, wagons, and tractors. Any small piece that belonged to a farm was wrapped each in a separate package, and each boy had one package a day to open. Great was the speculation as to what each package contained. The back ledge made an ideal place to set up the farm equipment. The boys rested on their knees on the car seat and spent many happy hours playing farm.

When they grew tired we all joined in various games. One of our old favorites is "Cities," described on page 264. It is interesting and surprising to note how quickly even the youngest child catches on to the sounds of the letters and soon becomes familiar with the names of many cities.

Another old standby that can be used for a car game is "My Grandmother." Someone starts off with some statement like "My Grandmother likes wasps but she doesn't like bees." The trick is for the following players to name objects not beginning with the letter "B" for her to like, and name others beginning with the letter "B" for her to dislike. In this case one could say, "My grandmother likes milk or honey or trees but she doesn't like bread or butter or black walnuts." Another basic sentence can start the game. "My grandmother likes coffee but not tea (T), or "My grandmother likes tomatoes but not peas (Ps)." For young children keep the words simple. The older children like to branch out a bit. This game makes the children very word conscious.

The "Color" game is always good. "I see something blue." Then the rest of the family name "blue" objects in the car. The one guessing the correct answer is "IT" and he'll probably choose some other color.

The youngsters like to play "I'm going to New York and take along—." The first player names something he'd like to take, the second repeats the first-named objects and adds one of his own, and so on around the group. Of course, the sillier the objects named the funnier the game, especially when the list gets long and involved.

When you think you'd like a little quiet in the car suggest that the first one that speaks is a "Monkey's tail." You'd be surprised how quiet small fry can be to avoid being a "Monkey's tail."

This is the pattern we follow when vacationing by car with the family. We have found that not only the youngsters but the oldsters as well thoroughly enjoy these family trips. So don't postpone that trip by car, waiting for the children to grow up. Always remember that nothing is more educational for all ages than travel.

FUN WHILE YOU MOTOR

We have found the following games delightful family entertainment while motoring through the country.

One of our party favorites is "Shopping." It is easily played in a car. You will find variations of it described on page 234.

Another excellent car game we call "Air, Water, and Fire." The one who is "IT" points to one of the players and calls out one of the three words "Air, Water, or Fire" and then quickly counts to ten. The player designated must name an animal living in the element called; unless the word "Fire" is called, then he makes no answer. For instance in answer to "Air" a player can say "blue jay" or "dog." If he fails to answer correctly before ten is counted or if he mentions an animal another player has already mentioned, he then becomes "IT." This game is lots of fun and educational as well because eventually a great many animals are named and their habitats learned.

There are several variations of the game of "Cities" which we have described on page 256. Another version of the same game is to restrict the names of the cities or towns used to a specific state or country. Everyone learns a lot of geography with this game.

A spelling match in the car is always fun. The spelling master chooses any two letters of the alphabet, for instance

"F" and "D," announces them and says that "F" will be indicated by the spellers raising the right hand and "D" the left hand. Then the master pronounces the words trying always to pronounce as many words as possible containing "F" and "D." To spell the word "Ford" the speller raised his right hand for "F," then says "O" and "R" and raises his left hand for "D." After a bit of practice the spellers can use more difficult words and more signs. Take the word "find." For "F" raise the right hand, *say* "I N," for "D" raise the left hand. For the letter "I" touch the eye, for "U" point to the spelling master, for "R" whistle, and for "S" nod the head. The player who misses becomes the next spelling master.

Another game that is exciting is a word builder. The first player starts off with a two-letter word such as "he." The second player adds a letter, perhaps "t," to make the word "the." The third player adds still another letter, perhaps "n," making "then." The next player can add the letter "i," making the word "thine." And so on until no more letters can be added which will make another word. Then the next person in turn can choose another two-letter word to start another chain of words. It is surprising what long words can be built up in this way.

FUN FOR THE SICK CHILD

When your youngster is sick, whether he is recovering from a case of sniffles or convalescing from a more serious ailment, remember that play is as important for him while he is in bed as when he is well. According to the doctors, a child who is happily occupied recovers much faster than a child who is irked with having to stay in bed.

From a mother's standpoint we all know that a happy child is much easier to care for than an irritable one. If the youngster has something to do he won't be constantly calling for mother, and neither will he be wearing himself out with threshing about.

While doctors urge us to keep these convalescing youngsters happily busy they do not tell us how to do it. However, there are many excellent play materials right at hand in almost every home that can be put to use to keep Junior happy although in bed.

Before launching into any play activity for your sick youngster keep in mind certain basic principles. Because a sick child tires very easily it is better to give him too little to do rather than too much. A bed cluttered with toys is very confusing to the sick so it is better to give him only one thing at a time to do.

An excellent way of handling play material for the convalescent is to have a number of trays. For instance, a child might think he'd like to work on a puzzle. Then find after putting a piece or two together that he is tired. The tray can be set aside without disturbing the puzzle and can be given to him at another time to work on when he is rested.

Pick the type of play you give your child so that it will be within his strength and ability to handle. Nothing must be too exacting, for ill children seldom care to exert themselves.

Do not start any play activities until the youngster has had his morning bath and whatever attention he needs. If possible, it is wise to move the child to another bed for the day. Even a very young child will appreciate a change of scenery and surroundings. And incidentally it encourages better sleep if his night bed is not his daytime playground.

After the young invalid is all set for the day produce a magic hat. Father's old top hat will add a touch of magic, but any hat will do. Let the youngster draw one of the many slips you have prepared and put into the hat. When he reads the slip he has drawn, or you read it for him, he will know what his first activity for the day will be. These slips can contain this type of information: "You may play with your puzzle; you may have the paper dolls; or you may play with the surprise box." There should be enough slips in the hat to cover all types of activity needed for a full day. These same slips can be put back into the hat for another day.

The surprise box can be a shoe box covered with gay crepe paper in which you can put bits of things for a child to play with. Your own child's tastes will govern the contents of this box, of course. For a little girl bits of silk and lace to dress a doll are always a joy. I well remember a surprise box of my childhood given to me on Christmas.

It contained nothing more than odds and ends of materials and laces collected by the family from the scrap basket. It delighted my little girl's heart more than all the other expensive toys put together.

For a boy the surprise box can contain mosaic blocks, a new knife and some soap for carving, hammer and nails, and a saw to be used at a later date when he is up and about. He'll love looking at them and dreaming and planning about the things he'll be able to make later.

Perhaps the slip the child draws from the magic hat will say "You may draw a package from the grab bag." Be sure to have the grab bag ready into which you have put little boxes, spools, favors from parties, old Christmas cards and other odds and ends you have gathered up around the house which might afford a youngster a bit of fun.

A sick child always likes to watch things grow. An indoor garden can be fashioned from a heavy tar-paper box. A landscape scene can be arranged in a flat box with tiny slips of plants for borders, real grass growing in the center and tiny stepping stones. Grass seed will begin to sprout in three days and can be loads of fun for the youngster to watch.

Children like to watch bulbs grow, but for fast action grow a carrot top. Scoop out the inside of a carrot about half way down. Hang it by a string near the bed and keep some water in it. It will sprout new greenery in a hurry.

That favorite of our childhood, a Cinderella garden, is fun for a youngster and simple to make. Soak in clear water a large coal or coke clinker or a number of small ones for several hours. Rinse thoroughly and place in a low flat bowl. Mix one cup of salt with two cups of water and pour the solution over the clinkers. The solution should be about one inch deep. Drop in a little mercurochrome, bluing or water-color paints for color. In a day or two crystals will begin to form and grow. More salt and water can be added later if needed.

If your youngster likes pets, and most of them do, try having a goldfish bowl nearby or a tiny turtle, or a tadpole or two in the bowl. Of course a bird is company too, but if you don't already have one it would run into more money than these other pets I have mentioned. Dogs are usually too active to have in the room, and cats are usually frowned upon as sickroom pets by the medicos.

If the child must have medicine on schedule, make a medicine clock out of a paper plate. Use cardboard hands secured with a metal paper fastener. Then set the hands on the medicine clock at the time when the next dose is to be taken. Place near this a real clock. When the hands on the real clock coincide with those on the medicine clock, even a rebellious youngster will think it fun to remind you that it's medicine time. At least he'll be mentally prepared for the visit of bottle and spoon.

A play clock can be made in a similar manner. Perhaps the invalid will enjoy making this second clock himself. On this clock set the hands ahead every hour. When the real clock catches up to the play clock the young patient will enjoy an automatic change of occupation.

Another interesting sickroom adjunct is a bulletin board. This needs to be no more than a large sheet of paper on the wall. On it post messages for the doctor, news from Dad's office, and cartoons snipped from the current papers or magazines.

And don't forget pinwheels or windmills. They are lots of fun for young patients. Take a piece of colored construction paper about four inches square and cut or tear from each corner to within three-fourths of an inch of the center. Pick up on the end of a pin—piercing from the back to the front—four alternate half corners. After you have the four half corners on the pin, put the point through the exact center of the paper and mount the wheel on the end of a stick or against some flat surface where the wind will make it whirl. The eraser end of a pencil is a good spot on which to stick your windmill.

Youngsters will spend oodles of time blowing the windmill, or the wind will blow it if it is fastened in an open window. To add variety to the windmill making, let the child use white paper and color designs on the square before it is pinned into shape.

Young children love "Finger Fairies." They can be drawn or traced on heavy white paper. Two fingers are inserted into the holes in the body to take the place of legs. You can make the finger fairy walk or dance up your arm or over the bedspread. And the fairy can tell Junior it is time for this or that. As soon as the youngsters get acquainted with your finger fairies they'll want some of their own. Draw one for the young invalid, except that you make the holes to fit his fingers. He'll love marching it up and down.

The mailman can help you with your sick child too. Drop postal cards in the mail addressed to the invalid. If you have time and the knack you can write little letters or draw funny pictures for the bed-ridden one—then mail them. They'll be ever so much more interesting if they come through the mail. The arrival of the mailman will help break the day's monotony.

Let your imagination run riot. When you enter the sick-room don't always be just plain Mother. Be a lady coming to call or the garbage man stopping in for a chat. Before you know it Junior will become another person—maybe a king or a queen, and you'll have to curtsy when you enter the room. Chuckles will greet you instead of whines if you catch his fancy in this game.

The radio can be your child's friend, but for Heaven's

sake watch what programs he is listening to or he may wear himself out listening to too many thriller-dillers.

Beside the puzzle we spoke of there are many kinds of handwork that are diverting. All of this equipment can be served on trays as needed. Scissors and paste, modeling clay, crayons, paper dolls, mosaic blocks, soap for carving, and doll furniture. The doll furniture can be made by the youngster or for the youngster out of safety-match boxes and cardboard and heavy paper.

Whatever you do, don't fail to be proud of the results of Junior's efforts. Even though his work turns out to be very poor, remember that he needs encouragement and praise. It doesn't matter how well he carves a horse, what counts is that he is busy carving.

When mealtime rolls around be sure that the helpings on his plate are small. It's very discouraging to face a big plate of food when your appetite is skittish. It's easy to fold a sheet of paper and pin it tepee fashion to set over his plate. He'll think it lots more fun eating a meal the Indians left.

Here's hoping all your children will stay well, but if they should be laid up don't let the worry and work keep you from bringing play activities to the child. For a busy child is a happy child, and a happy child recovers more quickly.

FUN AT A PICNIC

Does your family enjoy a picnic? Is there any better way to enjoy the balmy air and bright sunshine than to get the family, and perhaps some congenial friends, together in some pleasant spot out of doors, lay aside your dignity, along with your town clothes and join the children in a real frolic with some good things to eat thrown in?

The lunch need not be an elaborate one because the enchantment of the outdoors makes the simplest food delicious. Roasted potatoes, sweet corn roasted in the husks, and steaks grilled over the open fire never fail to please, or if you are not the boy-or-girl-scout type, and do not enjoy outdoor cooking, the food can all be prepared at home. Good old potato salad with deviled eggs, hearty sandwiches and fruit are always easy to serve.

A true and tried way to prevent too many fist fights and too many duckings in the creek by the younger members of the crowd is to keep them busy with games planned ahead of time.

On the way to the picnic ground usually excitement prevails. To calm the younger members of the family and to ease that sense of tenseness, we divide our carload into two teams. One team watches the right-hand side of the road and the other the left. The teams count cows, winning one point for every cow seen except for the white ones which count five points. This keeps the children busy, and busy children are not restless. To add spice to the game for the older youngsters we have a ruling that whenever a member of one team sees a white horse on the opponent's side of the road, it cancels all the opponent's points, and that side must start over again. Usually a total of 100 or 150 points is agreed upon as game.

If our chosen picnic spot is so secluded that we must hike through the woods to reach it, we play the game by giving one point for every tree of a certain variety seen and five points for something special. For instance, in our locality we award one point for every spruce spotted, and five points for every white birch. This is a most fascinating game and incidentally teaches the children to be observing.

Right after our picnic lunch we try to have a game that is not too active and still exciting enough to interest even the most energetic. "Air, Water, and Fire," mentioned before on page 267, is quite a favorite with us. Many times we have played it as a car game while motoring through the country. Here, at the picnic spot, all but one of the entire group sit in a circle. The extra player stands inside the circle and throws a small ball or knotted handkerchief at someone and at the same time calls out one of the three words, "Air, Water, or Fire," and then quickly counts to ten. The player at whom this was thrown must name an animal living in the element called; or if the word "Fire" is called, there must be no response. If he fails to answer correctly before ten is counted; or if he mentions an animal that another player has already named, he must change places with the thrower.

After this game the youngsters and oldsters as well are ready for a more active game. "Duck on Rock" is loads of fun to play out in the open. Each player must have a bean bag, which is called his duck. A large rock or a stump is chosen as the duck rock and twenty-five feet from it a line is drawn. Each player throws his duck from this line. The one whose duck falls nearest the rock becomes the first guard. He lays his duck on the rock and stands by it.

The other players then stand behind the line and take turns in throwing their ducks at the duck on the rock, trying to knock it off. After each throw a player must recover his own duck and run home (back of the line). If he is tagged by the guard while trying to do this, he must change places with the guard. The guard may tag him whenever he is in front of the line, unless he stands with his foot on his own duck where it fell. He may stand thus as long as he wishes, awaiting a chance to run home; but the moment he lifts his duck from the ground or takes his foot from it, he may be tagged. He is not allowed to lay his duck on the ground again after he has once lifted it to run.

The guard must not tag any player unless his own duck is on the rock. If it has been knocked off, he must pick it up and replace it before he may chase anyone. This replacing gives the thrower who knocked it off some time to recover his own duck and run home. As long as the guard's duck stays on the rock, several throwers may have to wait before they can try to recover their ducks.

A player tagged by the guard must put his own duck on the rock and become guard. The one who is no longer guard must get his duck from the rock and run for the line as quickly as possible, because he can now be tagged as soon as the new duck is on the rock.

If a duck falls very near the rock without knocking the guard's duck off, the guard may challenge its thrower by calling "Span!" This gives him time to measure with his hand the distance between the rock and that duck. If the distance is shown to be less than a span (the distance from the end of the thumb to the end of the little finger), the thrower must change places with the guard as if he had been tagged.

"Duck on Rock" is especially good for family groups because it does not entail running great distances and even the most rotund can compete. Also strategy enters in to such an extent that adult strategy can often offset youthful agility.

If your family is a musical one a nice way to end a picnic and to calm everyone down before starting home is to sing a group of songs around the camp fire. But if singing isn't your forte, perhaps your family would enjoy going "Shopping." As you may have read on page 242, a player who is the shopper walks around, stops before one of the group, and says, "I'm going to Denver. What can I buy?" He then counts to ten. Before he finishes counting, the player before whom he is standing must name three objects that begin with "D" (as dolls, dresses, and daisies). If he fails, he must take the place of the shopper. Any city may be named. However, the things to be bought must always begin with the same letter with which the name of the city begins.

The purchases that pop into one's head might be a revealing study for some psychiatrist, so if there is one in your group you'd better sing songs instead. Many times the most staid member of the family will purchase the weirdest assortment of objects, much to everyone's amusement.

I hope you enjoy your picnic.

SHARE YOUR VACATION PLANNING

More than half the fun of a vacation trip is in anticipation; especially if your family has youngsters in it. At least, that's the way it is with us. If the whole family becomes interested in a coming vacation the trip itself is more enjoyable for everyone concerned. We try to bring our travel interests out of the abstract into the concrete long before vacation time arrives.

When our third-grader comes home from school and says, "We're learning about Indians," he starts something. When he tells of some of the interesting things he has learned of Indian lore someone pipes up, "What fun to visit an Indian reservation this summer!" At that the bars are down. Opinions fly thick and fast in good old family style.

After days of discussion, pro and con, we agree that a trip to the Navajo country would be fun—that land of fifteen million acres where tall men and graceful women weave the famous Navajo rugs.

The fascinating pastime of gathering information is on. Daddy brings home travel folders from the railroad and plane companies that tell how best to reach the Navajo country. Jim, our oldest, who is history conscious, brings home library books on background stories of this

Indian tribe. Sometimes we read these stories and sometimes Jim reads them and tells us about them.

Fourteen-year-old Bob, the family mathematician, looks up the various routes by which a present-day family can visit the colorful Navajos. He then figures mileages and costs. He compares the advantages of travel by plane, by rail, or by car. He finds out the various scenic spots to be found on the way.

Grandma, whose interest is music, looks up old Indian songs and brings to us either in record form or piano music some of these songs that we can hear and learn. Closely connected with the Indian songs are the Indian dances and legends. The younger boys love to beat out the Indian rhythms on the drum. Not to omit anything we learn some Indian war calls and let the youngsters whoop it up (when they are in the basement).

We discover that our public library has an extensive Indian display in their museum. We find fascinating Indian relics at the museum of our State University. Trips to museums are so much more fun for youngsters if they have a definite purpose in making the visit.

A forth-coming birthday brings a gift of a stereoscope with a set of third dimensional pictures of the Indian country. The entire family from the oldest to the youngest enjoy looking at these and they make an ideal quiet-time activity for the youngsters.

Incidentally we find our travel interest a help during a siege of chicken pox. The youngsters cut out from the various travel circulars we have accumulated pictures illustrating our vacation trip-to-be, and paste them into an inexpensive scrap book. They print or write under each picture a few facts concerning the picture.

When the question of clothes for the trip arises Tommy is all for wearing only Indian feathers and war paint. However, with the help of the older boys we are able to persuade him to dress more in keeping with the white man.

We plan our wardrobe with an eye on the season and the climate, of course, but more than that we try to be travel wise and take only clothes that will pack compactly and will not wrinkle too much. If you are traveling with boys this is fairly easy. Polo shirts with either long or short sleeves as well as "T" shirts can be packed into an unbelievably small space. This leaves more space for the few dress shirts and other necessary clothing.

By this time our family is so well informed and so enthusiastic about the Navajo Indian that when summer comes the entire group is all set for the well-planned vacation. The travel time will not be dull or tiresome to the younger children because they will be aware of what to look for. A child is a poor traveler only when he is bored and time hangs heavy on his hands. A well-planned and discussed trip makes even a young child interested in the changing scenes.

For the year when our budget just can't squeeze out a vacation trip we use our travel technique for family fun on a different scale. For instance, a trip delightful to think about might be a trip to the moon. Silly you say? Not a bit of it. A family of youngsters is always highly interested in the sky world. Such a trip was the beginning of our Jim's interest in astronomy. We got books from the library that introduced us to the heavens. The boys were delighted to find the big dipper, the little dipper, Bruin, and the various other constellations.

Of course, Bob couldn't figure the cost of such a trip, but our mathematician got a kick out of computing distances, the speed of the rockets and the time it would take to reach the moon if such a rocket could go all the way.

Our astronomical interest took us to the University for views of the heavens through their telescope. The youngsters learned of Chicago's planetarium which we were fortunate enough to visit at a later time. If a trip to the moon ever does become an actuality I'm afraid our youngsters will be clamoring to go, for their interest in the sky world is very real.

Whether we plan an imaginary trip or some honest-to-goodness one, we have found that there is no more satisfying family fun than getting ready for it. Our vacation fun is really threefold; the fun of planning and anticipating, the actual trip, and the reminiscing during the following weeks and months.

285

286